Yorkshire Witches

Yorkshire Witches

Eileen Rennison

AMBERLEY

She war despert cross-e'ed, whal her snoot an' her chin,
Sed d'ye ya deea, ti t'tweea teeth wivin;
Her naals tha war lang, an' hump'd war her back,
An' baith lugs war pointed, her skin ommaist black;
Sha'd lang beeany arms, wiv a heead leyke a mop;
Tho baith legs war bent, she war wick ez a lop;
If she cam' leyke a snahl, leyke a wezil she'd gan,
An' sha oppenly traaded wi t'devil, did Nan.

– Description of a witch from Richard Blakeborough's
famous dialect poem 'T'Hunt o'Yatton Brig'.

First published 2012

Amberley Publishing
The Hill, Stroud
Gloucestershire, GL5 4EP

www.amberleybooks.com

British Library Cataloguing in Publication Data.
A catalogue record for this book is available from the British Library.

ISBN 978 1 4456 0292 9

Typeset in 10pt on 12pt Sabon.
Typesetting and Origination by Amberley Publishing.
Printed in the UK.

Contents

Introduction

We no longer believe in witches as our ancestors once did. We no longer fear them in the same way. Suggest that someone has bewitched you today and it will be taken as a compliment; it's a means of saying how charming and pleasant you have found them. But once it would have been an accusation that could have led to death by hanging or burning; occasionally both. When a witch was hanged and her body burned, it was done to destroy the great power she supposedly possessed, which could otherwise linger in a place after her death.

Witchcraft, with all its magical, supernatural power and knowledge, was believed to be practised by those – usually women, but also sometimes men – who were in league with the Devil or evil demons. Belief in the Devil was very strong in the medieval Church and witchcraft was regarded as heresy. Suspected witches were subjected to the Inquisition. By 1434, a great persecution had begun. Those found guilty were executed, often by burning. Confessions were obtained under torture, thereby reinforcing belief in the reality of witchcraft. The Reformation of the sixteenth century saw no diminution in belief in the Devil and the power of witches, his followers. Protestants believed in the existence of witches as much as the Catholic Church did, if not more. The great reformer Martin Luther declared in the 1520s that 'It cannot be denied but that the Devil liveth, yea, and reigneth throughout the whole world'. And, where the Devil had a foothold, then there were sure to be witches.

In 1431, the great French heroine Joan of Arc was burned as a witch by the English, and between 1484 and 1782 it is estimated that as many as 300,000 supposed witches were put to death in Europe. A huge number of these were in Germany. Ironically on 1 May, *Walpurgis Nacht* is now celebrated in that country as the Witches' Night in the same light-hearted way that we in Britain celebrate Halloween.

However, England and Scotland are also shamefully well represented in the roll call of European countries where witches were persecuted. Matthew Hopkins, the so-called 'Witchfinder-General', flourished in East Anglia during the Civil War and was responsible for the deaths of several hundred alleged witches in little more than two years. In the previous century, there may not have been as many executions but there were plenty of people who were accused and prosecuted. In fact, during the forty-five years of the reign of Elizabeth I there were more prosecutions than throughout the entire seventeenth century.

Many of these cases occurred in the county of Yorkshire. Indeed, the small market town of Pocklington in the East Riding of Yorkshire seems to have been something of a centre for witchcraft, and in 1630 earned itself the dubious distinction of being the place where the last witch burning in England occurred. The usual penalty in England was by hanging but not all supposed witches were punished by death. The Witchcraft Act of 1562 laid down the penalty of hanging only for witchcraft with intent to kill or destroy. For intent to hurt or destroy goods, one year's imprisonment was considered sufficient and six hours in the stocks was the prescribed punishment for lesser deeds. An Act of 1604, introduced soon after the death of Elizabeth and the accession of James I, who had himself written a book called *Daemonologie* in which he wrote of 'the fearefull aboundinge at this time in this countrie, of these detestable slaves of the Devil, the Witches or

Witch post in Ryedale Folk Museum, Hutton-le-Hole. (*Lucinda Rennison*)

enchaunters', kept the penalty of hanging for extreme cases. It was not until 1736 that an Act was passed that took the death penalty for witchcraft off the statute book. Even then, witchcraft – or (in those more enlightened times) the pretence of witchcraft, sorcery and enchantment – although no longer a capital offence, was still illegal and subject to fines and imprisonment. The law stayed on the statute book until 1951. Indeed, the last prosecution under it took place in 1944. That year, a medium named Helen Duncan was famously jailed under the 1736 Act for supposedly summoning spirits.

What exactly were witches? In the sixteenth and seventeenth centuries, when belief in the phenomenon was at its height, any unforeseen or unexplained event was liable to be attributed to witchcraft, and many communities contained a person who was regarded as a witch. Witches were believed to be capable, by means of spells and potions, of causing death and injury to individuals. They were said to be able to raise storms, blight crops and cause sickness in livestock. Sometimes they were thought to indulge in sexual intercourse with the Devil, and with his aid to obtain ill-gotten wealth. They were credited with the ability to fly and to transform themselves into animals. They were often said to have knowledge of future events.

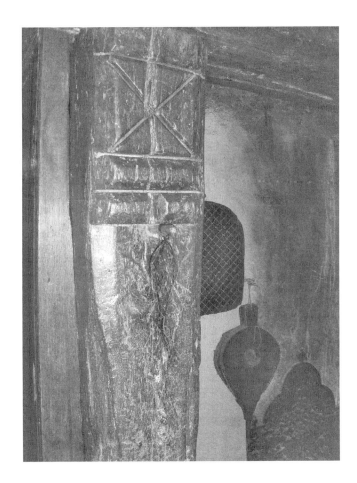

Detail of the witch post
in Ryedale Folk Museum.
(*Lucinda Rennison*)

A seventeenth-century woodcut of Matthew Hopkins, the so-called Witchfinder-General.

In the face of disasters, illnesses and any misfortune that they lacked the knowledge to explain, it is perhaps not surprising that people in the past looked around for a scapegoat. Inevitably, suspicion fell on anyone who was different. While most alleged witches were probably normal, some may have been insane, old and demented. Some may have had psychological problems such as hysteria. Any eccentricity of lifestyle or manner could lead to accusations of witchcraft. Physical appearance too seems to have been an influence and the ugly were often cruelly targeted. On other occasions, it is clear from surviving records that simple malice played the major role in initiating accusations.

The signs of witchcraft, people at the time thought, were clear to see if only you took the trouble to look. Witches were said to have marks of the Devil on their bodies as a result of their contact with him, and so a birthmark, a mole or even a scar, which today would be seen as entirely innocuous, could then be regarded with suspicion.

A rowan tree.

There were other indications as well. If someone touched a corpse and it bled that was a sure sign that they were a witch. On the other hand, causing a witch to bleed by even so small an injury as a prick or a scratch would take away or lessen her powers.

When people harboured such beliefs and fears, it is no surprise that they sought to defend themselves in any way possible from the evil powers of witches, and that they placed their trust in protections that were as irrational as the imagined threat itself. The rowan tree was regarded as a tree with powerful magical properties, and a twig of it placed over the doorway of house or farm building acted as a guard against witches. As late as the early twentieth century it was not unknown for people who presumably no longer believed in witchcraft to carry a piece of rowan wood in their pockets in the hope that it would bring them good luck. Iron, too, was thought to have powers to keep one safe from witchcraft, and discarded iron horseshoes were nailed over doors, giving a double benefit from both the iron nail and the shoe. These may still be seen over doorways, and today's brides are presented with symbolic horseshoes. Like the pieces of rowan wood, these have now been transformed into nothing more than good luck talismans. The colourful glass balls, which can often be found in antique and junk shops, are known as witch balls, and are bought today as pretty decorations. Once they were hung in windows in the hope of keeping the household free from witchery. In East Yorkshire, stones with a hole through them, which can be found on the Holderness beaches, were considered to have protective power and were strung on a thread to be used in the same way.

Peculiar to Yorkshire are the mysterious witch posts. These are wooden posts of rowan or oak, carved with a cross and other symbols, and built into the house, often as support for the smoke hood of the fireplace. Of only nineteen known examples, eighteen are from the North York Moors with the exception being found in Lancashire. The Ryedale Folk Museum at Hutton-Le Hole on the edge of the moors has a splendid example in a rebuilt moorland cottage. Others have found their way into the Pitt Rivers Museum in Oxford and the Whitby Museum. No one knows for sure what their purpose was, but it is generally accepted that they were there to guard the house from witches endeavouring to gain entry via the chimney.

The stories of the individuals in the following pages show how superstition and prejudice played an important and powerful part in the lives of the populace of Yorkshire from very early days up until more recent times, and led to the unhappiness and death of many innocent and harmless souls. The book is organized in alphabetical order of the witches it discusses, although there is a timeline at the end that shows their chronological order. Each story is self-contained, although certain recurring themes and ideas can be readily traced from one story to another. Readers can read the book from cover to cover or they can browse through it, reading a story here and a story there. Whichever way you read it, I hope that you will find that it contains plenty of interesting and intriguing material about the witches who have called Yorkshire their home county.

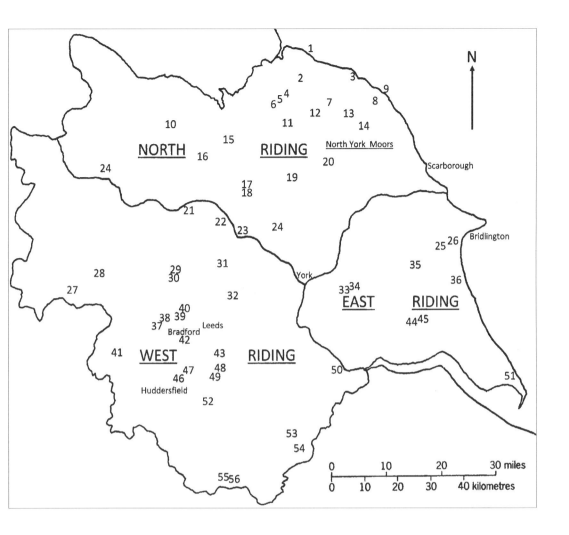

Map Locations

1 Marske
2 Guisborough
3 Hinderwell
4 Roseberry Topping
5 Great Ayton
6 Stokesley
7 Danby Dale
8 Ruswarp
9 Whitby
10 Richmond
11 Bilsdale
12 Westerdale
13 Glaisdale
14 Goathland
15 Northallerton
16 Leeming
17 Thirsk
18 Sowerby
19 Rievaulx
20 Hutton-le-Hole
21 Kirkby Malzeard
22 Ripon
23 Boroughbridge
24 Alne
25 Burton Agnes
26 Haisthorpe
27 Gisburn
28 Gargrave
29 Swinsty Reservoir
30 Timble
31 Knaresborough
32 Collingham
33 Barmby Moor
34 Pocklington
35 Driffield
36 Bonwick
37 Wilsden
38 Baildon
39 Idle
40 Yeadon
41 Heptonstall
42 Bowling
43 Rothwell
44 Bishop Burton
45 Beverley
46 Mirfield
47 Heckmondwike
48 Newton
49 Wakefield
50 Goole
51 Holpton
52 Woolley
53 Doncaster
54 Rossington
55 Sheffield
56 Woodhouse

Mary Bateman, the Yorkshire Witch

Even as late as the eighteenth and early nineteenth century, it seems that people were prepared to believe in witches. Mary Bateman, who earned for herself the title of 'the Yorkshire Witch', was able to convince people that she had supernatural powers; however, she was in fact a confidence trickster, a thief and a compulsive liar. Finally, she was a murderer.

Mary Harker, the daughter of a farmer, was born in 1768 in the village of Topcliffe near Thirsk. She was well educated for someone of her station and was able to read, write and do arithmetic, but she appears to have had little moral guidance. At the age of thirteen she went into domestic service in Thirsk, but was very soon dismissed for pilfering. Other jobs followed, all of them short-lived. By 1788, Mary was living in Marsh Lane in Leeds. She was working as a dressmaker, telling fortunes and claiming to have supernatural powers.

Mary married a wheelwright, John Bateman, after knowing him for only three weeks. Bateman also came from Thirsk, and he and Mary had three daughters and a son who was also called John. Marriage did not change Mary. Even her husband became a victim of her dishonest ways. On one occasion she took a letter to John's work purporting to report that his father was very ill. When he responded to the letter by hurriedly departing for Thirsk she proceeded to sell all his clothes and the furniture to pay off a victim who was threatening her with the Law. Her husband must presumably have forgiven her, but whether he was aware of all her frauds and dishonesty is not known. His involvement in his wife's assorted scams and double-dealings was never proved, but he must surely have been aware of what was going on and shared in the proceeds.

Mary wanted the same fine things as the ladies whose servants she made dresses for and she was prepared to use theft and fraud to that end. After a serious fire in Leeds she begged in the streets for money and blankets. Supposedly these were to go to the unfortunate victims but, in reality, they were for Mary herself. On another occasion she claimed to have a hen that laid eggs with the words 'Christ is coming' on them and charged people a penny to see her produce them from under the bird. She is said to have made a considerable amount of money in this way. We may think that her victims must have been exceptionally gullible, but this was an age when ordinary men and women had little or no education. In addition, Mary does seem to have had a great ability as an actress and special powers of persuasion, and she made full use of them.

She invented a helper named Mrs Moore who supposedly had the supernatural power to solve all the future problems of the people who consulted her, most of which were actually invented by Mary in her fortune telling. Mrs Moore, of course, had to be paid! By this means one poor woman was reduced to poverty in the attempt to avert the stream of terrible events that Mary foretold, and tried to commit suicide. She was but one of many who fell for Mary's fraudulent ways. In 1803, a Quaker family of a mother and two daughters who lived above their draper's shop in St Peter's Square in Quarry Hill mysteriously died within the space of ten days after taking potions provided by Mary. Their deaths were put down to cholera, the symptoms of which are very similar to those of poisoning. Mary, however, spread the story that it was the plague that had killed the three women, ensuring that everyone kept well away from the house for fear of infection while she plundered it of its contents. Surprisingly, no inquest was held and little or no suspicion seems to have been raised.

Mary's reputation grew in Leeds not only as a fortune-teller, but also as one who could ward off evil, a healer, and a witch. In her role as a healer she invented another helper in 1806, a Mrs Blythe, who lived in Scarborough and, by means of letters, advised her and prescribed medicines. And of course, like Mrs Moore, Mrs Blythe had to be paid.

Despite all these and other equally serious incidents, amazingly Mary managed to escape the attentions of the authorities for many years. Her luck finally ran out when she became involved over a period of time in mercilessly fleecing a Mr William and Mrs Rebecca Perigo of Bramley, Leeds. Armed with instructions from Mrs Blythe, Mary pretended to undertake the curing of the frequent chest pains from which Mrs Perigo suffered. Mrs Perigo was also complaining of being haunted by a black dog and other spirits. She had been told by her doctor, Dr Curzley, who was clearly as superstitious as his patients, that she was under a spell and that he could do nothing for her. A visiting niece suggested that perhaps Mary Bateman could help her, and so she was contacted. The meeting between the two women was to end in tragedy. Mary first asked for an undergarment of Mrs Perigo's to send to the non-existent Mrs Blythe and was given a flannel petticoat. A letter, purporting to come from the mysterious Mrs Blythe and posted in Scarborough, but actually written by Mary herself, duly arrived. It instructed Mary to go to the house of the Perigos and sew four guineas that she had sent into the four corners of Mrs Perigo's bed where they were to stay until told otherwise. Although he never saw the supposed money, which was hidden in silken bags, Mr Perigo was to provide an equivalent sum to return to Mrs Blythe in exchange for what she had sent. Trustingly but foolishly, he did so.

Letters, allegedly from Mrs Blythe, arrived in Bramley at weekly intervals. They always made requests for goods of various kinds and they always contained strict instructions for the letter to be burnt after reading, thus destroying the evidence. In this way Mary took more money, a cheese, tea, sugar and some china and silverware from the Perigos. There was even a request for a bed and bedclothes under the pretext that Mrs Blythe could not sleep in her own bed due to the spirits she was fighting on behalf of Mrs Perigo. After handing over gifts and money, the Perigos finally received a letter from Mrs Blythe advising them to eat puddings, which Mary Bateman would provide. Although the Perigos, of course, did not know this, Mary had added poison to them. Her victims were told that, without the puddings, which were made to a recipe provided by Mrs Blythe, they were both destined to die in the near future of a terrible disease. The puddings tasted vile and Mr Perigo could only eat a very small amount. His wife, however, managed to eat all of hers and soon died in agony. And yet, despite her death, it was only after two more years of being fleeced that Mr Perigo finally came to his senses. He ripped open the feather bed into which Mary had sewn the silken purses of money as part of the spell, to be retrieved at a time of her choosing. He found only pieces of paper and a farthing, and had Mary arrested. Many of the Perigos' goods were found in the Batemans' house together with quantities of Mercuric Chloride. This very poisonous substance produced symptoms that were consistent with those displayed by the Perigos when they ate the puddings. Mary was charged with Mrs Perigo's murder and committed to the Lent Assizes at York Castle on 17 March 1809 before Judge Sir Simon Le Blanc. John Bateman was also arrested but acquitted. Thorough investigation found no Mrs Blythe in Scarborough and forensic evidence showed traces of the poison in a remnant of honey given to Mr Perigo to be used with the puddings Mary had provided. The jury very quickly found the defendant guilty of fraud and murder.

She lied to the end, claiming her innocence, swindling a fellow convict while in prison, and also falsely stating that she was pregnant in an attempt to escape being hanged. A panel of older experienced women was immediately formed to examine her and declared that she was not with child. On 20 March she was executed outside York Castle by William 'Mutton' Curry. (His nickname had been given him because he had been convicted of stealing sheep but reprieved on condition that he took on the job of hangman. He carried out the grisly duties from 1802 to 1835.) The hanging took place before a huge crowd of 5,000, some of whom, still believing in her supernatural powers as a witch, waited expectantly for her to use her magical powers to escape death. Over the weekend before her execution Mary wrote a letter to her husband, in which she admitted some of her crimes but not the murder. She sent him her wedding ring and asked him to give it to their daughter. After her execution Mary's body was taken to Leeds Royal Infirmary for dissection. People paid three pence each to view the body and £30 was raised for the Infirmary. Strips of her skin were also sold as gruesome souvenirs. Mary did not escape the hangman, but in one sense perhaps, she did not die for she is still remembered, and her skeleton can still be seen in Leeds Medical Museum.

Jennet and George Benton, 1656

In the 1650s, Jennet Benton lived with her son George in a mud-walled, thatched cottage in the village of Newton, between Stanley and Wakefield. She had the reputation of being a witch whose powers of sorcery and enchantment derived from an alliance with the Devil. The fact that Jennet had a fierce black cat that hissed and spat at anyone who approached no doubt reinforced this idea. The belief that witches kept such creatures as 'familiars', which were agents of the Devil, was a common one at the time.

The Bentons were in constant dispute with Richard Jackson, tenant of nearby Bunny Hall Farm, about their trespassing on his land. They insisted that they had a right-of-way. He denied this and eventually gave orders to one of his men, Daniel Craven, to stop them if they continued to cross his farm. Shortly afterwards Daniel caught them doing so and endeavoured to carry out his orders. In doing so, he became involved in a fight with George Benton. George picked up a stone and threw it at Daniel. It was not a large stone but it caught him full in the mouth with the result that Daniel lost two teeth and sustained a cut lip. George Benton was taken to court, accused of assault and trespass, and ordered to pay compensation to Daniel.

Justice seemed to have been done and the matter settled. Mr Jackson must have felt that he had been vindicated with regard to the trespassing and must have hoped that there would be an end to it. The Bentons would simply accept the verdict of the court. This was not to be. Afterwards, a disgruntled Jennet Benton threatened Richard Jackson, saying, 'it should be a deare days worke … to him or to his before the yeare went out'. Following this threat, Mrs Jackson lost her hearing, one of the children took a fit in the night and Jackson himself was racked with pains, heard strange noises and suffered other misfortunes. Remembering her words, he was convinced all his woes were due to bewitchment by Jennet Benton and he accused her of witchcraft at the York Assizes on 7 June 1656.

In his evidence, Jackson described how, in a fit, he was surrounded by the noise of music and dancing, which was not heard by anyone else. The following night, he was tormented by the sound of bells, together with music, dancing and heavy groans, but neither his wife nor his servant could hear anything. When pressed they finally agreed that they did hear three loud groans. Then the dogs howled at the windows as if they were ready to tear Jackson and his wife to bits if only they could get in. The noise caused the herd of pigs to panic and break out through the barn doors, the house doors banged and rattled, furniture moved about unaided, and ghostly black cats and dogs ran around in the house. Furthermore, eighteen of his horses and mares had died within the year. This was an unusually high number to die of natural causes. They must have been bewitched, he believed, by Jennet Benton.

Susanna Maude, the wife of Robert Maude of Snow Hill, testified that Jennet Benton came one day to her house seeking her son. When Jennet asked him if he would go home with her, Susanna said that he replied, 'Mother which way shall I go?' and added, 'You know I can goe thorrow the stone wall if yow would have me.' She also told the court that either his father or the Devil had been to her house and struck the iron range with the fire tongs making a loud ringing noise at all times of the night. Jennet's response to that was to ask, 'Did it ever doe thee any hurt? It will do so at the noone time.'

The jury listened to all this, but apparently were not convinced by it. The Bentons denied everything and were acquitted. In spite of the superstition, fear and belief in witchcraft, which was so strong during this period, it seems that there were times when common sense prevailed.

This case is an example of what was a regular occurrence throughout the seventeenth century in which a poor villager was accused of witchcraft by a richer one. It also perfectly demonstrates the sort of neighbourly quarrel that could lead to threats, and these in turn generated the accusation of witchcraft should misfortunes occur. In an earlier case in July 1611, Elizabeth Cooke, a bad-tempered woman who quarrelled with her neighbours, was prosecuted as a witch at Thirsk in the North Riding. She was accused of having threatened and cursed her neighbours and their goods. The Justices dismissed the case, saying quarrels between neighbours were not uncommon, and many people said in anger things that they did not mean. Once again, as in the case of the Bentons, we see an accusation of witchcraft arising from neighbours quarrelling, and the Yorkshire common sense of the Justices in dealing with it.

Isabella Billington of Pocklington

We tend to think of burning as the penalty for witchcraft, but the normal and most frequent method of executing witches was hanging. Isabella Billington, a thirty-two-year-old housewife of Pocklington – a small market town in the East Riding of Yorkshire – has the dubious distinction of having been both hanged and burned. Many people at the time considered that the power of witchcraft lived on after death, and could only be extinguished by fire. Because of this belief, in some cases, after death by strangulation, the body of a witch would also be burned. Isabella Billington's crime was of such a repulsive and incomprehensible nature it may have been thought that her powers were so strong that they merited this double penalty. On 5 January 1649, together with her husband, she had crucified her mother, and then sacrificed a cockerel and a calf as a burnt offering to the Devil. Presumably they imagined themselves to be undertaking some ritual of the dark arts, but we do not know exactly what their purpose was.

The busy scene today of Pocklington Market Place where the mob burned Old Mother Green in 1630. (*Graham Eagland*)

The stone on the Knavesmire in York which marks the spot where hangings took place. (*Graham Eagland*)

The couple were imprisoned at York Castle, tried, and sentenced to death at the Lent Assizes. When the day of execution arrived, the castle records describe a huge crowd gathering outside the prison. Twenty-one people were to be executed at the same time. Of these fourteen were men, all of whom had been found guilty of treason and faced hanging and disembowelment – the usual penalty for that crime. The crimes of the seven women included arson and murder for which they were to be hanged. Only Isabella was sentenced for the crime of witchcraft and suffered both hanging and burning. The name of her husband does not appear in the records at this particular point and it would seem that he was executed at a different date.

On the day of this multiple execution, the jeering, howling mob blocked Castlegate, making it almost impossible for the procession of prisoners to get through, and followed it through the town and out of the city through Micklegate Bar to the Knavesmire, where executions took place at that time. In this period of the Civil War, which culminated in the execution of King Charles I only weeks after Isabella had committed her crime, it is possible that the hostility of the crowd was directed against authority and the soldiers accompanying and guarding this miserable parade. At least some there that day may have been in sympathy with the fourteen men as they were dragged along on sledges, with the seven women following behind in rattling carts. But whatever the motive and mood of the mob it must surely have added to the fear of the already terrified and wretched prisoners, who sang psalms throughout the journey, presumably to comfort and fortify themselves for what lay ahead. For the crowds on this terrible day in York it was an exciting event with the added edge of horror – a gruesome entertainment even. For Isabella Billington it was a truly horrible end, but no more so than the one she had inflicted on her own mother.

Richard and Isabel Breare, 1652

Witchcraft in Yorkshire, and indeed in England, was a somewhat dull and prosaic affair compared to the ways in which it was seen on the Continent. English witches were not thought to indulge in wild and dissolute orgies and eat the flesh of babies or to fly to midnight Sabbats with the Devil, as many claimed their European counterparts did. The first recorded allegation of a witch flying seems to have come from Roger Nowell, during the examination of the Pendle witches in Lancashire in 1612, when Jennet Preston was said to have flown to a meeting at Malkin Tower. Later, in 1621, Edward Fairfax accused five women, the Timble witches, of attending a midnight gathering and feast presided over by the Devil – a Sabbat, but not one to which it is suggested that they flew. It is perhaps significant that both these men were educated gentlemen and could well have read books on witchcraft from the Continent that had influenced them.

While the idea that witches could fly became more generally accepted as time went on, it was a rare accusation in Yorkshire. Later it was more the stuff of village legend than any accusation that appeared in the court records. The idea of a coven of witches was not one to be found in our area, although accusations against more than one witch were not unknown. It was fairly common for two people to be accused of being involved together in a bewitching, but a case at Mirfield in the West Riding was unusual in that a group of six people were all accused of involvement in the same affair.

On 1 May 1652, three labourers: Richard Breare and his wife Isabel, Robert Tailer, his wife Anne, Francis Breare and a woman known only as Elizabeth, were said to have bewitched one Grace Allenson. As a result she weakened and wasted away until the beginning of September. What the nature of her impairment was and whether her recovery was gradual or her restoration to health on 1 September was miraculously sudden, we do not know. What her relationship was to the group, who seem likely to have been members of the same family, would have been interesting to know, but this information has been impossible to obtain. Since the accused were all of the labouring class, it is possible that Grace Allenson was their employer or at least of higher status, and that some class-based disagreement may have been behind the accusation. Isabel Breare seems to have felt some guilt – or perhaps it was simply fear – for she fled and left the other five accused to face the music. Despite the testimony of eleven witnesses, they were found not guilty. No doubt Isabel would have been had she remained.

Mabel Brigge, 1538

Mabel Brigge, a thirty-two-year-old widow of Holmpton in the Holderness area of East Yorkshire, was executed in 1538. Was she an innocent and humble pawn in the intrigues and private enmity between two better-off farming families? Did she, either willingly or not, take part in an attempt by one family to harm or blackmail the other without realising where it would lead her? Reading the testimonies at her trial of those involved it would seem so, yet Mabel alone was found guilty and suffered the ultimate price in a case that certainly involved local politics and, given the period, possibly religious undertones.

Her alleged crime was witchcraft in the form of a Black Fast, undertaken to do treasonous harm to the King and the Duke of Norfolk at the behest of Isabel Buck. Fasting at that time was a recognised religious act, usually of penitence, and in no way unusual. However, fasting to bring harm to another was a method employed by witches to aid concentration and was known as a Black Fast. It involved refraining from meat and milk and any food containing milk, with the witch concentrating her mind and willpower on the desired object for the duration of the fast.

There are a good many unanswered questions in the trial of Mabel Brigge, but the circumstances in the country at that time could explain why the authorities displayed such an extreme reaction to the case. She seems to have been tried under laws brought in after the Pilgrimage of Grace, the title given to a widespread revolt in late 1536 and early 1537 against Henry VIII, and his Dissolution of the Monasteries. In those two years, a number of revolts took place against the King in northern England, but specifically the title belongs to the rising that originated in Yorkshire between October and December 1536 under the leadership of Robert Aske, a Yorkshireman born in the East Riding.

Aske was assured of safe conduct by the King and the Duke of Norfolk to put the grievances of his followers to them and granted a pardon, but as soon as the rebel army was dispersed, the leaders of the Pilgrimage were arrested. Around 200 people were executed for their part in the rebellion and, in July 1537, Robert Aske was

Rysome Garth, where Mabel Brigge lived before moving to the Lokkars. (*Graham Eagland*)

hanged in chains in York. Abbots of the four largest monasteries in the North were also executed. It is therefore not surprising that the authorities in East Yorkshire were keen to show that they would come down hard on any supposed threat to the King. Henry's Queen, Jane Seymour, died on 25 October 1537, and they would not have wanted any suggestion to arise that witchcraft could have been involved in her death. Mabel Brigge would appear to have been doomed from the first, despite her constant claims of innocence, and testimony that seems to support her version of events. Both she and Isabel Buck, the other woman involved in the accusation, maintained throughout that the fast was only undertaken to recover money lost by Isabel.

Mabel Brigge made a statement to the examining authorities that Isabel Buck approached her on her way to church on Trinity Sunday and asked her how she was doing. She replied, 'but weakly' because 'her child that her living hang by was taken from her'. It is not clear what this remark refers to. Had she lost a child of her own by death or had she perhaps been dismissed as a nursemaid for someone else's child? The latter would explain the reference to her living but we do not know. Isabel then asked her to fast for her on a particular saint's day and, in return, she would give her a peck (a dry measure of two gallons) of wheat and half a yard of linen cloth. She said the fast was for the recovery of some money that she had lost, and assured Mabel that the chantry priest of Holmpton had given her his approval to do this. Sir Thomas Marshall, the priest, later confirmed this under examination. Fasts of this nature were often authorised by the Church to invoke the favour of a saint.

The evidence of Elizabeth Broune of Holmpton also seems to confirm this version of events. She stated that one day between Whit Sunday and Lammas (Wednesday 1 August 1537) as she was passing the house of John Buck with a basket of fish,

Isabel Buck asked her to give a message to Mabel Brigge to tell her to stop the fast, which she said she had asked her to do to find money that she had lost.

The Lokkars of Reysome Grange said Mabel Brigge had come to their house with two children a week before Lammas, and a message was sent immediately after by Nelson of Rysome Garth asking them to allow her to stay and he, Nelson, would 'see her costs paid'. Nelson does not appear to have been called to give testimony and we hear no more of him. Why he should pay her costs in another man's house is one of the many unanswered questions in the affair.

Agnes and John Lokkar noticed that Mabel fasted on the next Friday, Saturday and Sunday. They declared that, when they asked her why, she said it was a charitable fast. She also told them that she had once fasted for a man who broke his neck before the fast was over, and she trusted that the same would happen to the King and the false Duke 'that had made all this business'. Presumably this was a reference to the closing of the monasteries and to the turmoil caused by the Pilgrimage of Grace. She went on to say that she had been hired to do this by Isabel Buck.

However, in her testimony, Mabel says that this is what John Lokkar had asked her to say, promising to give her two shillings of his own money and get five shillings for her that Nelson owed her. He declared that Isabel and William Buck had enough and that it would help both him and her if she would agree to say this. If this were true then it would appear that John Lokkar was intent on harming the Bucks and that he hoped to obtain money from them by threatening to accuse Isabel publicly, using Mabel as the means to do so. He dismissed Mabel and went to see Isabel Buck. Isabel then confronted Mabel. She, of course, denied that she had fasted for anything but the return of Isabel's money and stated that she had never said otherwise. When Isabel told her husband, he and his father sent for John Lokkar to ask him not to take the matter any further, and gave him three shillings and two yards of linen cloth. Despite this gift (or bribe), Lokkar refused.

William Fisher of Wellwick testified that John Lokkar spoke to him around Michaelmas (25 September) and asked him to go to the Vicar of Holmpton to put on record his knowledge of Mabel Brigge's fasting. Fisher stated that she had been his servant and had fasted for five weeks, one day each week. At the end of the fast, she had said that all Holderness would be bound to pray for her and Isabel Buck. He went on to say that he had dismissed her under suspicion of stealing some money from a locked chest in his house, but she had denied it. He had beaten her with a staff.

The Vicar of Holmpton, Ralph Bell, testified that John and Agnes Lokkar had told him that Mabel Brigge had used a Black Fast against the King and the Duke of Norfolk, and that William Buck's wife Isabel had hired her to do it.

On 11 March 1538, all these persons, with the exception of Elizabeth Broune, were taken to York where they were kept in separate prisons and re-examined. All reaffirmed their previous testimonies. Agnes Lokkar added that Isabel and Mabel had sworn 'hand in hand, foot upon foot, and kissed upon the same' never to reveal the fast, not even in the confessional. Mabel seems to have confirmed this but she added that, if Buck had been surety for Lokkar for '£7 for kine unto John Wright of Holderness all this business would not have been'. This statement does seem to confirm the theory that the Lokkars had a quarrel with and a grievance against the Bucks, and had a motive for implicating them, callously using Mabel Brigge for their own ends. She was found guilty of witchcraft and swiftly executed, presenting us with one final unanswered question: Why was it that Mabel Brigge paid with her life yet Isabel Buck went free?

Molly Cass of Leeming

In the early 1800s, Molly Cass was notorious for causing trouble around the village of Leeming, where she lived in a tumbledown cottage near the mill. Everyone was afraid of her, so great were her powers and her reputation as a witch. There were those who swore that they had seen her riding her broomstick high above the mill near which she lived. Whenever anything was amiss Molly was suspected. She never found herself brought before the court – this was the early nineteenth century and witchcraft cases were things of the past – but she did not always escape punishment for her suspected misdeeds.

Such was the case with regard to the loss of Jane Herd's caul. A caul is a thin membrane sometimes covering the face of a baby at birth. It was considered to be lucky: the child would never hang or drown and would have special powers that they could use for good or ill. Sailors would pay a good price for a caul as a safeguard against drowning, but mothers often kept it to give to the child when old enough (as recently as the 1950s, when my son was born with a caul, the midwife asked me if I wanted to keep it).

Jane Herd used her caul for harmless social purposes. If she placed it on her bible and spoke the name of a friend, its power would call that person quickly to her door. Until one day it blew away out of an open window, much to Jane's distress. Although she ran outside at once and searched everywhere neither she nor those she called to help her could find it anywhere. Just to have lost it was bad enough but then things began to go sadly awry for Jane. Her sweetheart no longer seemed to love her and she developed a nasty swelling on her neck and another on her leg.

Jane could only suppose that someone had found her caul and was using its magic power against her. Help was sought from the wise men of nearby Bedale, Master Sadler and Thomas Spence. They put together certain strong-smelling ingredients and boiled them in a pan over a fire lit with rowan wood, the anti-witch wood. Jane was instructed to breathe in the fumes that arose from it and, with her hand on the bible, to speak the names of those that she thought might have her caul. The wise men kept a watchful eye on the boiling pan while Jane tried out a few names. Each one was declared innocent until Jane mentioned Molly Cass. Immediately the pan boiled over and filled the room with such foul-smelling fumes that everyone was forced to rush outside. There they found Molly Cass peering in at the window. She was seized and held inside the fume-filled room until she confessed that she had taken the caul. We do not know but can only suppose that Jane retrieved her caul. Molly was ducked nine times in the mill-race.

In another story told about her, Molly Cass plays a more benign role, acting as avenging angel for a person wronged. A certain George Winterfield of Leeming was refusing to marry the girl he had got pregnant. A wrathful Molly appeared one night as he and his friends were playing cards. She told him that the Devil had him and would never let him go. George was so frightened by her that he begged for a second chance and said that he would marry the girl. Molly declared that she seldom gave anyone a single chance let alone two. She told him 'the girl's waiting for thee George. She's asleep in the bulrushes. Go to her. All roads lead to the Swale tonight.' George hurried off immediately but he did not return that night. The next morning his body was found in the river and not far from that of his deserted sweetheart. She had drowned herself rather than face the shame of bearing an illegitimate child.

Did George also kill himself out of guilt on finding the girl? Or did Molly's powers somehow cause him to do so? She certainly seems to have known that the girl was to be found in the Swale, hence her remark to George about her sleeping in the bulrushes. But we do not know how she knew. Did she know through magic powers or had she simply seen her there?

Her uncanny ability to know things when it did not seem possible is illustrated in another smaller incident. Two men were quarrelling over the ownership of a cow and rather strangely went to Molly to try to settle the matter. Or so the story goes. Perhaps in fact she actually came across them quarrelling. However that may be, she told them to go home. The problem she said had been settled by a turnip. Mystified the men returned home to find the cow dead. It had choked on a turnip!

Elizabeth Creary, 1623

The early seventeenth century was a time when prosecutions for witchcraft were common throughout England. The King himself, James I, was a strong believer in the power of witches, although he also realised the difficulty of proof if brought to trial. North Yorkshire was one area where few cases of prosecution for witchcraft occurred. When they did the result was often acquittal. Whether this was due to tolerance on the part of the Justices, enlightened disbelief or simply lack of any real proof, we cannot say. Between the years of 1606 and 1657 only six such cases appear in the records of the North Riding Quarter Sessions, and none at all after that date.

One of these was the case of Elizabeth Creary, the wife of Thomas Creary of Northallerton, who was accused in October 1623 of 'exercising certain most wicked arts, enchantments and charms' on a black cow belonging to Edward Bell, a farmer of Northallerton. The cow was a valuable animal worth 50s and also in calf, but it was claimed to have been 'sorely damaged and the calf within her totally wasted and consumed' by Elizabeth's wicked enchantments.

There was to be no acquittal for Elizabeth. She was tried by a jury of yeomen and found guilty. Her punishment was to be 'committed to prison for a year, and once in each quarter to stand in some market town in the Riding upon some fair day or market day,' and on release 'to be bound to the good behaviour for a year and then appear at the next Sessions to stand to such further order as the court shall set down'. This does seem a very severe punishment. It is not clear, but the year in prison may perhaps have been conditional upon her good behaviour during the year in which she was to stand four times in the pillory. Perhaps the court considered her crime atoned for if that were the case, and the prison sentence was rescinded at her reappearance at the Sessions. Although such a punishment was not unknown elsewhere in the country, this was the only one of its kind recorded in the North Riding Quarter Sessions.

Elizabeth Crossley, 1646

The village of Heptonstall looks out over the Calder and Colden Valleys from its hilltop site above Hebden Bridge. Its gritstone cottages once housed handloom weavers. Its Cloth Hall was built *c.* 1550 by the Waterhouse family of Shibden Hall, and is the oldest one in Yorkshire. It was here that the weavers brought their cloth to sell in what was a thriving trade until the eighteenth century when Halifax increasingly became the centre for such wares. In 1643, the village became a garrison of Parliamentarians in the Civil War. On 1 November of that year attacking Cavaliers lost many lives, washed away in a storm. Others were lost when the Roundheads rolled boulders down on them. Royalists responded with reprisals in which some of the houses were burned.

Three years later, in 1646, when the village was presumably restored to peace, Elizabeth Crossley, a woman who had a reputation for witchcraft, called at the house of Henry Cockrofte, a clothier, begging for alms. She was not turned away empty-handed but it seems that whatever she was given did not please her, and she made this quite plain before she left.

Two nights after this event, William, the eighteen-month-old son of Henry Cockrofte, fell ill. Previously he had been fit and healthy but now he became very pale, arching his body and screeching as if in great pain, throughout the night. The child recovered but remained in less-than-robust health after this attack, and he became rather dull and stupid. Seven or eight weeks after the first episode, he had a recurrence of the same illness, which continued for about three weeks. Again he seemed to recover, but he had a relapse and died on 10 December, 'after hee hadd languished nyne or tenn dayes'. Henry Cockrofte was convinced that the child had been bewitched, and together with three other men – Samuel Midgley, Jonas Uttley and Lawrence Hay – he went to see Mary Midgley, whom he suspected of being a confederate of Elizabeth Crossley. Why he felt that she was the culprit rather than Elizabeth Crossley is not clear since it was definitely Crossley who had the grievance about the alms.

Whatever his reason, he accused Midgley of having bewitched his child, and after threatening her and striking her, he forced her into admitting that 'shee could witch a little.' Jonas Uttley corroborated this and Samuel Midgley (presumably not a relative) testified that although she had been struck he was 'verily persuaded that the confession was not made from fear but according to truth'. However, Mary Midgley went on to say that Elizabeth Crossley, her daughter Sarah, and Mary Kitchin were witches who had bewitched the child, and she would be prepared to swear it before any Justice in the country. It seems that whatever there might be amongst thieves, there was no honour amongst witches! As for herself, Mary Midgley now denied the charge of witchcraft. With her 'head sore broken' by Henry Cockrofte she had confessed, she said, 'in hopes to be freed from further blows'.

All this was brought out in depositions before Charles Fairfax and Thomas Thornhill, the Justices of the Peace, at the end of December 1646. Daniel Briggs of Waddsworth also added that an infant named John Shackleton had suffered similar 'paynes and convulcions', which had lasted for about three months. When the child was at a neighbour's house, the minister of Croston Chapel came to see him and warned those with him that, if they met anyone on the way home, 'they would longe or desyer to mawle them on the heade'. They did in fact meet Elizabeth Crossley and the maid carrying the child tried to avoid her. Elizabeth, however, asked how the boy was and seemed to be very angry when the maid simply said that he was not very well. Shortly afterwards Elizabeth Crossley was in the same house as the child and was struck by the maid with a candlestick, whereupon the child was well until the next day. Later he began to have the fits again and, after languishing for some eleven weeks, died.

The morning of his funeral, Daniel Briggs met Elizabeth Crossley who asked him if he had brought 'this witched childe to town'. When he replied that he thought that the child was not bewitched, she swore that he was. Daniel went on to give evidence that his mother on her deathbed about seven years before had said that she feared that she had been hurt by Elizabeth Crossley, who had a reputation as a witch.

Another man to give testimony, Richard Wood of Heptonstall, stated that four days before Midsummer Day of that year, Mary Midgley had come to his house to beg for wool. Perhaps she was hoping to earn something by spinning, but Mrs Wood told her that she had given her a good deal of wool three weeks before and would give her no more. She explained that they had to pay for their wool. She did give her some milk, but Mary was still very angry and left. The very next day six of the Wood's milk cows fell sick. Mrs Wood confronted Mary and accused her of hurting them and asked her to remedy it. Mary at first denied being involved but eventually confessed that she had done them some harm. On the receipt of sixpence from Mrs Wood, she told her to go home and to place a handful of salt and an old sickle under each cow. If they did not recover, she was to come to her again. The next day all was well and the strange charm seemed to have worked. When Richard Wood met Mary Midgley in the alehouse he mentioned that there had been a problem at his house that she had caused. She then gave him an apple and said that, although she had on several occasions hurt him, she would never do so again. All the women involved in this affair, when brought before the magistrates, denied ever practising witchcraft and no further action was taken. One surprising fact that emerges from this case is that some of the people involved seem to have had no great fear of the reputed witches. They were not only prepared to confront them but even to strike them, unconcerned that the supposed witches might retaliate. At the same time they were evidently of the opinion that Elizabeth Crossley and others had the power to cause death.

Katherine Earle, 1655

One day in 1654, a Mr Franke and Katherine Earle were drinking in an alehouse in Rothwell in the West Riding. Whether they were drinking together or were simply there at the same time, we do not know. Katherine was a married woman, the wife of a labourer, and so perhaps it was the latter. It does seem likely that they at least knew each other for Katherine greeted him with a very familiar remark. She clapped him on the shoulders, as one might well do in hearty greeting, and said, 'You're a pretty gentleman, will you kiss me?' Of course, she may have been offended that he would not kiss her and this rejection prompted the blow. Or maybe it was simply that Katherine was already slightly drunk.

Whatever her reason for clapping Mr Franke on the back, it was to lead to an accusation of witchcraft. When he died soon afterwards, she was said, through her touch, to have killed him by a spell. In January 1655, Katherine was brought before the authorities and charged with death by witchcraft. According to one source, she was duly executed; according to another, she is said to have been acquitted. She was certainly accused of other acts of witchcraft at the time. It was also alleged that she had killed the mare of Henry Hatfield by the same method. She had struck it with 'a docken stalk,' and, striking Hatfield as well, she had caused him to suffer great pains from which he 'dwindled, peaked and pined' for as much as six months afterwards. The accusation was supported by Mrs Hatfield, although her testimony cannot be relied on as unbiased. Katherine had earlier been employed by Henry. They had been lovers and Henry was believed to be the father of Katherine's daughter, Anne. Anne for her part does not seem to have had any daughterly feelings for him. Seeing his pain she asked, 'Doth the Devil nip thee in the neck?' and went on to warn, 'He will nip thee better yet.'

It was stated at the hearing that Katherine had been duly searched and found to have a mark on her body, 'in the likeness of a pap'. This was regarded as certain proof of a witch. The belief was that the witch suckled the Devil in the form of a 'familiar'. This was usually a dog or a cat but also sometimes a toad or other small creature. By so doing, the witch received her powers from him. Any mark or protuberance that could be imagined to serve or result from such suckling was taken as a sign. Any pet animal seen nuzzling against the body of a supposed witch was cited as further proof of the belief. It was usual for three or four respectable women to be given the task of examining the body of an accused witch and to report their findings to the magistrate.

Mary Sikes of Bowling on the outskirts of Bradford was one who was searched in this way in 1649 and found to have unfamiliar and wart-like lumps. Margaret Morton of Warmfield in the West Riding was another accused woman who was subjected to a similar search in the following year and was found to have two strange marks which were black with a blue centre. Very dark moles can often appear black and bluish in the centre and can be raised like warts, but they may well have appeared sufficiently strange and unknown to superstitious searchers for them to be identified as witch-marks. Anne Hunnam of Scarborough was also found to have an unusual protruding mark on her body when she was examined in 1651 by three women appointed by the Justices. These are just three examples of such cases and there are others. It seems obvious to us today that the women were simply unfortunate to have on their bodies some unusual wart, sebaceous cyst, wen, or birthmark but, in the mid-seventeenth century, they might pay for such slight disfigurement with their lives.

Peggy Flounders

In 1736, the laws on witchcraft in Britain were finally repealed. The Church by this time no longer regarded it as heresy and the Law no longer regarded it as a felony. However, the belief in witchcraft still lingered on amongst the uneducated populace. Since the Law and the Church no longer offered protection from witches or even acknowledged that they existed, village people turned to the so-called wise men and wise women. Their skills were also seen as based in the supernatural but they were used for good rather than evil purposes, and they included help in dealing with the problems caused by witchcraft. One such wise man was Jonathan Westwick of Upleatham near Marske in the North Riding of Yorkshire. Although a gamekeeper by occupation, he is recorded in the late eighteenth century as dealing with the problems caused by the Marske witch Peggy Flounders.

Peggy had come to the village as a young woman and she had three children born out of wedlock. A disreputable character, she nonetheless married Henry Flounders, a respectable market gardener who had lost his wife. She seemed set for a reformed life, but it was not to be. Henry disappeared soon after the marriage, either voluntarily or, possibly, as a victim of a press gang. Peggy continued to live alone in her cottage at the end of the village street, and, over time, her uncontrollable bad temper made her many enemies. Her strange, unprepossessing appearance and her unpleasant nature – as she grew older, she developed a beard – were no doubt instrumental in earning her the reputation of being a witch. Soon she was regarded as the initiator of anything unwelcome, unpleasant or inexplicable that occurred in the village. Certainly a farmer named Oughtred was in no doubt of who to blame when one night a loud knock came at the door, and the maid who opened it fled screaming that a monster was outside. Her master looked out but could see nothing and shut the door. He asked the maid what she had seen and sobbing she replied that it was a demon 'like a pig but all afire'. Immediately a loud crash was heard, and Mrs Oughtred's best china was discovered smashed to smithereens in the parlour next door.

More inexplicable breakages occurred, horses became lame and cows went sick and gave no milk. Farmer Oughtred was convinced that he had somehow offended Peggy Flounders and that she had sent a demon to plague him. He sought the help of Jonathan Westwick. Jonathan agreed with Farmer Oughtred's diagnosis of the cause of the problems and promised to remedy them with his own magic. This entailed closing and sealing all the doors and windows of the house, while a black fowl pierced by nine new pins was burned to a cinder on the fire. An incantation was chanted throughout the burning, which had to be complete by midnight. Those present were warned that, if they spoke of the ceremony to any outsider, the spell would not work. Jonathan's magic seems to have been successful. The Oughtred family had no more trouble.

Peggy would also on rare occasions lift her own spells. When one farmer left his farm a broken man due to cattle losses laid at Peggy's door, she met the new farmer with a smile and a blessing. She laid her cloak on the path and jumped over it, thus removing the spell she had previously cast over the farm. This incident suggests that she may have come to believe in her own powers, or perhaps simply enjoyed a malicious feeling of power over the villagers that her reputation gave her. Whatever Peggy Flounders' beliefs, it seems that the inhabitants of Marske were in no doubt of the existence of both malign and benign witchery and Jonathan Westwick had no shortage of people seeking his help.

There are records of at least two more occasions when he used his magic against the local witch. Hannah Rothwell and Mary Parker had both quarrelled with Peggy Flounders and so blamed her when Hannah's butter would not set and Mary's cow gave no milk. Jonathan's advice to Hannah was to thoroughly wash out her churn three times: the first time with boiling water with a handful of salt in it, the second time with boiling water containing rowan berries and the third time with plain boiling water. Then she was to drive into it two small plugs of rowan wood – a tree well known for its protection from witches – and to chant as she churned, 'This tahme it's thahn, T'next tahme it's mahn, An' mahn for ivver mair'. His advice to Mary was laxative and exercise for the cow. It was not to be milked for its full yield for nine days and on the tenth day before milking it normally she was to whisper in its ear the words 'Ah's milking tha foor Peggy Flounders'. He took the precaution of covering himself by stating that, if this did not work, then she should sell the beast as it was not bewitched at all. It was simply a poor animal.

Peggy Flounders died in 1835 aged eighty-five. She had been vilified throughout most of her life as a witch, but despite her reputation, she was given a Christian burial. She lies in the churchyard of St Germain's church, Marske.

Hester France

Hester France of Huddersfield was accused on 23 January 1652 of having cursed and bewitched Elizabeth Johnson, the servant of Hester Spivy. More than three hundred and fifty years later, the deposition made by Hester Spivy before Henry Tempest Esq. Justice of the Peace, presents us with several problems in making out exactly what had transpired to bring about this accusation.

Both Hester France and Hester Spivy were widows, but it would seem that Mrs Spivy occupied a somewhat higher social position. Not only was she able to employ a servant but she may well have been a mill owner. She states that on the day when this all began 'she went unto the milne' and was coming home at night. This suggests that this visit was rather more than a casual errand. If it had been, she would surely have sent her servant. When there was no son to take over a business, it was not unknown for a man to leave it to his wife to carry on and this might have been the case with the Spivy family. Mrs Spivy then goes on to say that Elizabeth Johnson told her that Hester France had been at her home when she, Elizabeth, had been mending the fire with the 'firepoite'. This seems likely to be a firepot, an earthenware pot used to carry a small amount of fire or combustible substance from one area to another to light or liven up a fire. In recent times of open fires it was common practice to carry a small quantity of burning coals on a shovel from a well-lit fire to light another in a different room. Hester France is then mysteriously reported to have said that 'it was a goode deede to seare her lipps with itt, if she thought anie thing by itt' before leaving the house. It is not clear what 'itt' is or whose lips are being referred to. Was Hester threatening Elizabeth with fire if she made anything of her being in the house? Or was she asking her for something to eat and suggesting it would be a good deed if Elizabeth gave it? Whatever this passage may mean, Hester then returned and cursed Elizabeth and 'prayed to God that she shold never bake againe'. This does seem to suggest that Elizabeth was baking and refused Hester anything. Elizabeth told Mrs Spivy that she thought Hester had bewitched her but was told that her mistress hoped she had better faith than to fear either witch or devil.

The next part of the deposition is equally puzzling. It states that Mrs Spivy was frightened by a great noise made by Elizabeth in the night as they slept. The next morning she sent her to some neighbours 'to see if her eare rootes were not downe, but they were not downe'. Did this have anything to do with the noise in the night and ears and hearing? Or, if the assumption of Mrs Spivy's connection with the mill is correct, perhaps it refers to something to do with ears of corn. The words of the deposition are not clear. Perhaps only a learned scholar of seventeenth-century language could explain them. What is not in doubt is that when Elizabeth returned from the neighbour's house, she took to her bed and could neither stand nor speak for the whole of that day, apart from one occasion when she spoke to her brother. Hester France was sent for. When she came, Elizabeth took hold of her, accused her of harming her and scratched her severely. Having done this, she felt somewhat better but still not entirely well.

Another witness testified that Hester France had been a reputed witch for more than twenty years. Yet another said that she had been reluctant to go to Elizabeth Johnson when he went to fetch her. John Jolinson of Huddersfield also testified against her saying that a man named Robert Cliff had been very weak and sick for six months. He had sent a message to the Constable of Huddersfield asking that Hester France be sent to see him. When she came he 'scratcht her very sore', and said that he believed that she was the one who had caused his illness. Hester denied this, saying that she had never hurt anyone in her life. Whether this helped Robert at all is not stated.

What became of Hester France is also not on record. She may have been acquitted. There are many things that are unclear about this case. It does, however, illustrate the belief that, if one drew the blood of a witch, even by as little as a scratch, one could diminish or completely destroy their power over one.

Susannah Gore, the Barrow Witch

Susannah Gore was reputed to have flown 'ower Driffield chotch (church) on a blazin' besom' when she died at the age of ninety in 1826. Another version of this magical and spectacular event says that it occurred when she sold her soul to the Devil, but quarrelled and fought with him in a house being built at Nafferton Slack. She pulled his nose and scratched his face, and together they all but demolished the house in their struggles.

Susannah was married to Thomas Gore, a paper manufacturer. Whether he was the owner of the business or simply an employee we do not know, but it would seem that his wife had her own profitable business. It was Susannah who in 1798 bought No. 1 Chapel Lane in Driffield for £58. After living there for four years, she sold it to the father of Joseph Barnett the weaver for £200. From Chapel Lane she went to live at Barrow where she earned her title of 'the Barrow Witch'. She does not appear to have stayed for a very long time in Barrow before she returned to Driffield, and in 1803 she built the house there now known as the Spread Eagle, which stands on the corner of Exchange Street and Eastgate. Nevertheless, it was as 'the Barrow Witch' that she continued to be known.

She was famous throughout the countryside for her power to see into the future, dispensing wisdom and advice on all manner of subjects to all manner of people. Young women came to her to know if their love affairs would lead to marriage, businessmen wanted to learn what the results of financial speculations would be and tradesmen hoped to hear of improvements in their businesses. Parents with absent children sought reassurance that all was well with them, and the superstitious came to hear whether their ghostly figures had been seen entering the church on St Mark's Eve, a sign of approaching death. The church was easily seen from Susannah Gore's house and she kept watch. Help in locating and retrieving lost or stolen property was also a common request.

When a wealthy farmer had a bag containing a hundred guineas stolen from him and all efforts to discover the thief were to no avail, he rode over from Skipsea to

Is this the porch that Susannah Gore
watched from her house in Church
Lane on St Mark's Eve? (*Graham
Eagland*)

The house which Susannah Gore built in Driffield in 1803, now the Spread Eagle pub. (*Graham
Eagland*)

consult Susannah. She told him not to worry about his loss for the money would very soon be returned to him. If it was not back within the week he was to visit her again. The very next morning he found the bag with all the money intact hanging on his door sneck. It had been returned by the thief in the night. All Skipsea knew of the farmer's mission to Driffield and it would appear that Susannah's reputation alone was sufficient to convince the thief that his exposure was inevitable. Such incidents, of course, added to her reputation and increased belief in her powers.

As we have seen, whatever she did was always intended to help people, not to do harm, and so she should perhaps have more accurately been known as a wise woman. But it was as a witch that she was always known and, because of this, the children of Driffield were afraid to pass her house or to meet her in the street.

Hannah Green, the Lingbob Witch

Witches were usually poor women, widows living from hand to mouth and often dependent for food or alms on the goodwill (or sometimes the fear) of the people amongst whom they lived. Hannah Green was a notable exception. When she died in May 1810 she left more than £1,000, a veritable fortune in those days. She was popularly known as the Lingbob Witch. *Lingbob* in the local dialect means Heather End and is near Wilsden. Today there is a Lingbob pub in Wilsden, although this particular building, built in 1836, could not have been where Hannah Green lived; however, an older one once stood on what is the present pub car park. There was a small hamlet of old cottages in the vicinity, one of which Hannah is likely to have lived in. She painted her chimney stack white so that her clients would have no difficulty in finding her. She later moved to a cottage on the edge of the moors on the old road from Otley to Bradford, between Carlton and Yeadon.

She was said to be able to transform herself into the shape of many different creatures, but her favourite, as is the case with many witches, was the hare. In this form she got up to many nocturnal tricks and, according to one improbable story, she was shot and killed by an unsuspecting poacher, who himself almost passed away with fright at the sound of her terrible dying screams. In reality she died in her bed in 1810 at Yeadon. She was married to a miller and had a daughter, also named Hannah, who claimed to have the same skills after her mother's death but had little success.

Hannah Senior's special magic skill lay in being able to predict future events both in the wider world and also in the lives of individuals. Foretelling the future for people was the source of Hannah's wealth but whether she charged a set fee or was rewarded with a generous donation we do not know. What is known is that her fame was such that people came from considerable distances to consult her and even the carriages of the gentry were often to be seen at her door.

Like horoscopes in newspapers and magazines today, her predictions for individuals were always vague and couched in terms that could be interpreted to cover the most probable events of their lives. When it came to world events she was slightly more specific, giving dates and predictions, which those who believed in her powers might well, with hindsight, connect to actual historical events.

In 1785, a gentleman from Sheffield paid Hannah a visit out of curiosity in order to see what she could tell him of the future of a relative in prison. He was told that trouble would continue for 'three times three years' but then would come 'a great deliverance'. This apparently fitted accurately with what the gentleman knew of the matter and so he was prompted to ask if she could tell him what might be about to occur in the wider world. She assured him that she could and first of all mentioned a war that would 'blaze out in all its horrors' and spread to all neighbouring countries. Two countries far apart would, however, obtain their freedom as a result of this war. After 1790 many great persons, even royalty, would lose their lives but 'not by fair means'. In 1794, a great warrior would fall in battle and, in the following year, a people who had been 'dragged from their own country' would rise up and free themselves from their oppressors.

It is easy to see how her believers could later see these predictions as references to the French Revolution, the Napoleonic Wars and the uprising of the slaves in Haiti led by Toussaint L'Ouverture. Cynics might say that all these events were, in her vague descriptions, the sort that were always likely to be happening somewhere in the world. It would need only two or three to fit her predictions by coincidence for Hannah's reputation to remain intact. Be that as it may, Hannah Green practised her art of prescience successfully for forty years and in the process she became a wealthy woman.

Ann Greene, 1653

The village of Gargrave is one of the largest in the District of Craven in North Yorkshire. It lies on the edge of the Yorkshire Dales National Park, 4 miles north-west of Skipton, and is a popular venue for hikers and cyclists. The River Aire runs through it, dividing it in two, and it is unusual in having not one village green but five.

In the mid-seventeenth century Gargrave had a different kind of green – a woman living there named Ann Greene who was accused of being a witch. On 16 February 1653, John Tatterson testified before John Assheton and Roger Coats, the local magistrates, that a fortnight after the previous Christmas he was unwell. He did not say what exactly ailed him but simply stated that he was 'disabled in body'. It seems that his illness was not merely physical as he goes on to say that one night when he was in his father's house he was 'troubled with ill spirits' who tried to persuade him to worship the Devil. These spirits were all invisible 'saveinge Ann Greene'. Though they tormented him more than four times, he called on the name of the Lord and was able to resist their persuasion. Despite the fact that he claimed that she had been one of the spirits who appeared to him, he then went to see Ann Greene, telling her that he had pain in his ear and he thought she could help him. Ann said that the remedy for earache was black wool but John seems to have regarded what he had as more than a simple earache and said that 'that was not the matter'. Nevertheless, Ann removed her garter (presumably of black wool) and passed it across his left ear three times. At the same time she got some hair from his neck without his permission. When he asked her what she wanted it for she told him it was no business of his and he was to go home and not bother about it. As he went home the pain in his ear became worse. He returned to Ann and threatened her, saying she should 'looke to itt or hee would looke to her'. She repeated the business with her garter and promised that the pain would be gone. After a discharge of matter came from it, Tatterson's ear was indeed well again.

Jenett Hudson, also of Gargrave, testified that Ann Greene had told her that John Tatterson was 'overgone with ill-tongues and that he should have one side taken

A corner of Gargrave village today. (*Graham Eagland*)

from him'. The meaning of this remark is not entirely clear. It could have been a threat to disable him on one side of his body made in response to John Tatterson's ill-natured threat to Ann when she was trying to help him. This was undoubtedly why the comment was put forward and entered in evidence against her. But equally it could have been just an angry remark about his unpleasant attitude and words, and she was referring to a side of him that needed improvement.

Testimony against Ann was also given by Margaret Wade, who said that her daughter Elizabeth, when in bed one night, had begun to cry loudly. She went to her to see what was wrong and Elizabeth told her that she saw a huge bitch with a dish in her mouth sitting on the end of her bed. On another occasions Elizabeth reported having seen three creatures 'like blacke dogges' that came around her bed. She identified two of them as local women, one of whom was Ann Greene. They tormented her by pricking her in her side and head. It seems strange that the girl was able to identify her night-time visitors as the women she named if they appeared in the form of dogs. No one else seems to have suggested that Ann Greene could change into animal form, though it was generally believed that many witches were able to do this.

In fact, Ann might more accurately be regarded as a wise woman than a witch. When she was called to defend herself, she freely admitted that she did sometimes use a charm to deal with earache. She explained that she had used it twice in one night for John Tatterson, passing her garter over his ear while asking the ancient god Boate nine times for his help. For pain in the head she would need a lock of hair and some of the sufferer's water, which she would boil together and then throw into the fire. She declared that she never attempted to cure any other type of ailment. She was found not guilty and was presumably free to continue to try to help others more grateful than John Tatterson.

Nan Hardwick

Nan Hardwick lived in the small isolated community of Spittlehouses in Danby Dale on the North York Moors. Although we cannot be certain it seems very probable that she was the daughter of Matthew Hardwick, born in 1765. What is certain is that she was well remembered by the elderly parishioners of Canon Atkinson, the Vicar of Danby, who recorded their memories of her in the middle decades of the nineteenth century. She was not the only witch recorded in Danby Dale but she was the most famous.

One story told of her begins with her begging at a farm in nearby Westerdale, where she was given some bread and beer, which she seems to have accepted with gratitude and thanks. The farmer's wife was pregnant with their first child and due soon to give birth. Nan looked in on her and informed her that the baby would be a boy and would be born before the next morning. 'Thoo'll call him Tommy, won't tha?' she said but was told that, if the baby was a boy, the parents planned to call him John. 'Ah but tha'd best call him Tommy,' was Nan's reply before she bade them 'Good day' and left. Sure enough, as Nan had predicted, the wife went into labour later that day. The farmer set off with his horse and gig to fetch his wife's sister, who lived 5 miles away, to help with the birth. He had not gone far when the horse stopped and refused to cross a bridge. He tried to get down in order to lead it across but he found that he could not move. His immediate thought was that Nan might be involved and, although he could not see her, he called out to ask her what it was that she wanted.

She was still nowhere to be seen but he heard her laugh and her reply, 'Thoo'll call the bairn Tommy or thoo'll not move a step further.' What was the poor man to do? It was a strong superstitious custom that once a name had been settled on it must not be changed. To do otherwise would bring bad luck. But he had to get quickly to his sister-in-law or who knew what might happen to his wife and the baby with no one there to help her. Of course, he agreed that the baby would be called Tommy. Both he and the horse were freed from their paralysis and he was able to continue his journey. Whether he kept his word we do not know but, if not, he no doubt would have had Nan to deal with. This story seems to suggest that Nan took a gleeful pleasure in her ability to do such things, for there seems to be no real reason for what she did. She had been well received at the farm and given food and drink. She just seems to have been determined to have her way and would not be denied it.

Another story shows Nan using her powers to retaliate to an unkind and insulting remark. She had walked 20 miles from Spittlehouses to a place called Lowna Bridge where she had relatives. She arrived on the day of the wedding of the daughter of the house. There were so many guests staying the night that it was impossible to find a bed for her. One of the bridesmaids kindly offered to share her bed with her. When she was told this, the bride remarked that she wouldn't fancy having that old hag in bed with *her*. Unfortunately, Nan overheard her and not unnaturally was offended. She declared that, if she wouldn't sleep with her, she'd not sleep with her bridegroom that night. In the celebrations and boisterous horseplay among the young men following the wedding the bridegroom fell off a ladder and broke his leg. As a result Nan's words came true. Whether by chance or magic powers, who can tell?

Yet another story tells of her using her powers to make a person unable to move. In this case the trick was used against Thomas Prudom who was one of the overseers of the Parish Relief Fund. When Nan had applied to him for financial help he had refused her saying that she was not sufficiently in need. Shortly afterwards, as he returned home from Castleton, he met Nan at the little bridge crossing the stream that runs through the dale. The bridge was narrow with no room for two people to pass. Although Nan had already set foot on the bridge Prudom arrogantly stepped onto it at his end. He obviously thought that a prosperous farmer like himself took precedence over a little old woman like Nan and expected her to retreat. Instead he suddenly found himself rooted to the ground, unable to move or to speak. And there he stood until Nan felt inclined to relent and free him.

We shall never know whether Nan Hardwick really did have special powers or whether her reputation was built on chance happenings that seemed to fulfil her words. Certainly the people of Danby Dale believed that she was a witch with magic powers, and to have such a reputation was perhaps enough to cause strange things to happen.

Mary Hartley and Bridget Goldsbrough, 1736

The first statute against witchcraft was passed in 1542 during the reign of Henry VIII. It outlawed the use of magic to discover buried treasure, together with the making of love charms and causing harm to any persons 'through witchcrafts, enchantments or sorceries'. The penalty was forfeiture of property and death but this law was little-used and was repealed in 1547. In 1563, during the reign of Elizabeth I, another law was passed, much the same as the earlier act, except that the new one stipulated a year's imprisonment as the penalty for a first offence and the death sentence only after a second offence. In 1603, James I came to the throne and a new law against witchcraft was passed the following year. This one tightened up the law by making the first offence of harm by witchcraft a capital offence. This remained the law until 1736 when witchcraft ceased to be a capital offence in England.

In effect, this meant that the Law no longer believed in witchcraft but there is no doubt that belief in and fear of witches lingered on in the minds of many ordinary people. In November 1736, just a few months after the repeal of the law, a case came up at the Quarter Sessions concerning two women in the village of Baildon in the West Riding near the Lancashire border. Mary Hartley accused Bridget Goldsbrough of turning into a grey cat and bewitching her son, saying that she should 'let my bairn alone, he works hard for his living, and cannot bear to be disturbed at night'. She claimed that the night before Bridget had 'ridden her son to Pendle Hill'. Margaret Goldsbrough, Bridget's daughter, was also a witch according to Mary Hartley. The younger Goldsbrough was also intent on riding Mary's son like a horse. She had brought a bridle and saddle and would have 'put the bridle in his mouth but the bitts were too large'. This refers to the belief that witches were given to riding at midnight to their Sabbat or coven (a belief actually more common on the Continent) and would use a bewitched person in this way. It is from this belief that we get the term 'hag-ridden', which came to mean tormented by nightmares or, eventually, driven by obsessions. Her mention of the famous

Pendle witch case in 1612, over the border in Lancashire, indicates the strength of the witchcraft tradition among the common people. It was at Pendle that the first suggestion arose in this country of witches gathering in a coven, and more than a century later the hill was still obviously regarded by some as a meeting place for witches.

This accusation led to a heated altercation in the streets of Baildon. Witnesses described how Mary Hartley berated and accused the two Goldsbrough women, joined in this by her husband John and another family member known as Red John. All three of them, the witnesses said, shouted 'kill them all and let them live no longer', as well as other unspecified 'dangerous language'. This case is interesting in that it was not about the accusation against the Goldsbroughs. It was actually brought by the Goldsbroughs against the Hartleys and resulted in the latter family being bound over to keep the peace. The authorities by this date had changed their attitude to witchcraft as this case clearly shows.

Susan Hinchcliffe, 1674

When someone was accused of witchcraft it usually seemed that the whole community was against them. If the accusation arose from fear and ignorance, it is understandable as these feelings were often shared by very nearly everybody in the community. However, many accusations, it is now apparent to us, were caused by malice or by a 'falling out' between neighbours. One would have thought, in these cases, that there would be friends or relatives who would support the accused. Yet seldom do we find anyone who stands up for the accused and defends them. They may, of course, have feared having the same accusations directed at them.

However, there were cases in which voices were raised on behalf of the accused. In the case of the Timble witches in 1621, six women were accused by Edward Fairfax of bewitching his daughters. Henry Graves, the Vicar of Fewston, testified to their good name and they were acquitted. His standing in the community as a man of the cloth no doubt had a bearing on the verdict. Even more strikingly, when Mary Moor of Clayton accused Susan Hinchcliffe, before the magistrate Henry Darcy Wentworth at Woolley in the West Riding on 26 August 1674, no less than fifty respectable citizens gave her their support in a petition testifying that she was 'unblameable in every respect'. This was quite extraordinary, but sadly it did not have the effect that one would have expected and the case did not turn out as well as that of the Timble witches. Mary Moor was a girl of sixteen and her testimony consisted entirely of conversations she claimed to have heard between Susan Hinchcliffe, the wife of Joseph Hinchcliffe, and her daughter Ann Shillito, the wife of Thomas Shillito, both of Denby.

First of all Mary said that Susan had told Ann that, if she could persuade Thomas Haigh to buy threepennyworth of a certain substance and look him in the eye when he gave it to her and touch his hair, 'we shall have power enough to take life'. She also asked Ann to go to help with the hay at Thomas Haigh's and bring home in her mouth nine bits of bread and nine bits of butter. This unlikely achievement she claimed would give them power to kill his stock, and declared that the Haighs would not be so grand then for they would leave them neither cow nor horse. Ann then asked her mother if she had harmed Mrs Haigh. Susan replied that she had indeed, by touching the edging of her skirts and thus making her unable to walk.

Mary then went on to claim that, on another occasion, she had heard Susan tell Ann that she was unable to achieve her ends with a certain Thomas Bramhall. He had so much wicken (rowan wood, a supposed guard against witches) about him that she had no power over him and would have to give up. Susan then went on to ask Ann if she had heard how Timothy Haigh had almost drowned in the dyke. When Ann said she had not heard, Susan told her that she had had him in her power when he was riding up and down the moor and she had intended that he should either break his neck or drown. His horse had thrown him off the bridge but he had then managed to get back over the bridge to Susan's surprise. She thought it could only have been with the help of the Lord, but she went on to declare, 'next time lett the horse and him look both to themselves'. According to Mary, she then heard Ann ask Susan if she had done any harm to John Moor. Susan said that she had caused two of his pigs to die and made his child ill. She also told Ann that if her father had only touched Martha Haigh before she had spoken to him they could have had power over her to be able to take her life.

Mary Moor then proceeded indirectly to implicate Joseph Hinchcliffe, Susan's husband, in his wife's and daughter's activities by saying that, in the middle of July that year, she had overheard Ann Shillito tell her mother of a piece of magic that she had seen her father do which had amazed her. He had required butter and it had instantly appeared on his knee in a little wooden saucer. Her mother replied that that was nothing, asking her, 'Hast thou lived in this house soe long and never saw none of thy father's tricks?' She then told her how her husband had once gone to get shoes from a man named John Walker. Walker had refused to let Hinchcliffe have them without money, and 'he never made pair after'. The same thing occurred to George Coppley when he refused Hinchcliffe cloth without payment – 'he never made peice att affter but two'. Susan then, according to Mary, told Ann that, if anyone would not let them have what they wanted, they were prepared to take that person's life, and that her father was as bad as they were but kept it well hidden. He only did these things 'farr off'. Ann then said that, if it became known what they did, they might be hanged. Susan told her that no hemp rope would be able to hang them. When her daughter feared then that they might be burnt, Susan reassured her that they would tell nothing until they died and so would never be found out. Ann replied that she was sure that her mother would say nothing and admit nothing even if she came before the magistrates.

In all this testimony, Mary Moor gives the impression of a person who has launched herself on the telling of something and cannot resist adding to it and elaborating it. Nowhere does she say how she came to overhear so many conversations or how it was that she alone appears to have done so. Either she was adept at eavesdropping or the Hinchcliffes were singularly open and unguarded in their talk, especially when, according to Mary Moor, they had so much to hide. If the latter was the case it seems strange that no one else heard anything or spoke out against Susan Hinchcliffe and Ann Shillito; on the contrary, as already mentioned, a petition made and sworn to by fifty people who said that they 'never heard or had the least ground to suspect her or her said daughter, to be in any sort guilty of so foule a crime, but do fully believe that the said information against them both is a most gross and groundless (if not malitious) prosecution'. As for Mary Moor, they added that 'some of us could say too much concerning her, of quite different nature, but that we judge recrimination to be but an indirect way of clearing the innocent'.

Astonishingly, in spite of all this, Susan Hinchcliffe and her husband were bound over to appear at the next Assizes. Ann would seem to have been dismissed from the charge. There is no record of the case at the Assizes, but a different source says that the affair so preyed upon the mind of Joseph Hinchcliffe that, on Thursday 4 February 1675, he went into a nearby wood and hanged himself. His body was not found until the Sunday and in the meantime his wife had also died. From what cause we do not know, but it was reported that she prayed for her accuser on her deathbed.

Anne Hunnam or Marchant, 1652

Often in cases of witchcraft the accused is said to have caused the victim to have a fit or fits. This sometimes seems to be just a general term, indicating only that the person in question had been taken ill. At other times it appears to be used in the same way that it is today when we refer to an epileptic fit. In a case in Scarborough in which Anne Hunnam (also known as Marchant) was accused of bewitching the three- or four-year-old daughter of John Allen, two witnesses gave detailed descriptions of the fits suffered by the child. They seem to be describing very strong convulsive fits that may well have been of an epileptic nature.

Marjery Ffish, a widow, declared under oath before the bailiff Luke Robinson, that the child had six fits in an hour when she was present. She went on to describe how during the fits the hands and arms were 'drawne together contracted, the mouth some tyme drawn together, other tymes drawne to a wonderful widenesse, the eyes drawne wide open and the toung rite out of the mouth (almost bitten of), looks black and the head drawes to one side, the mouth drawn aurye, and makes noise, with trembling; and when itt is out of the fitts starts often as in feare'. Mrs Ffish believed that the child was bewitched. We can assume that Mrs Allen, the child's mother, also held that belief, since she took advice to send for Elizabeth Hodgson, who was reputed to be able to use charms against bewitchment. When Elizabeth came, she told Mrs Allen that the child had been bewitched by a glance from Anne Hunnam as she passed the father carrying his daughter in the street on their way home from Scarborough fair. She also said that the child would be recovered by midnight. When this did indeed seem to have happened, Mrs Allen told Mrs Ffish of Elizabeth Hodgson's visit, of her accusation against Anne Hunnam and of the good news of her daughter's recovery. Sadly, what was assumed to be a cure turned out to be nothing but a temporary respite. Elizabeth Hodgson claimed that, although she had indeed cured the child before, she was now unfortunately incurable because her mother had not kept Elizabeth's role a secret. This demand for secrecy was a useful ploy by charmers to cover themselves when their magic failed. It gave them an excuse and an opportunity to pass on the blame to another. Human nature being what it is, people like Elizabeth could be pretty sure that the secret of the consultation would not necessarily be kept. It would be almost impossible not to confide in one's spouse, another family member or even a close friend.

Mary Weston also gave testimony before Luke Robinson. She told him that she had been sent by her mistress, Anne Smallwood, to sit with the Allens' daughter through the night. She mentions another woman being present – perhaps Marjery Ffish who seems to have been closely involved with the family – but does not give a name to this second person present or suggest that it was Mrs Allen. It may be that she had been sent there in order to give Mrs Allen a much needed rest. She stated that the child had the surprising number of forty fits during the night and went on to describe them in very similar terms to those used by Marjery Ffish. She describes the child 'sometimes drawne together in a rounde little lump', and sometimes stretched out so stiffly that she and the other woman 'could not bend her'. She also notes the drawn-up hands and knees, the wide-open mouth with tongue hanging out, the staring eyes and head drawn to one side, but adds that blood came out of the mouth. As Marjery Ffish mentioned the tongue almost bitten off, it seems likely that that was the source of the blood.

Marjery Ffish, Elizabeth Dale and Elizabeth Jackson were then set to examine the body of Anne Hunnam for any signs of a 'witch mark'. This they did, and they testified on oath to having found such evidence in the form of a blue wart-like spot. Confusingly, it was said by Marjery Ffish to be on her left side and by Elizabeth Dale on her left buttock, but both women agreed that, when pricked by a pin, it was insensitive to pain. This was believed to be a sure sign of a witch, being the means by which the Devil or 'familiar' sucked the blood and the witch received in turn her magic powers.

However, when Anne Hunnam herself was questioned, she denied having hurt the child by witchcraft or in any other way and denied practising, 'any conjuracions, witchcraft or evil intents'. As the judicial records do not give any indication that Anne Hunnam received any punishment, we can only suppose that she was acquitted of the charge.

Alice Huson and Doll Bilby, 1664

Even in the 1600s, when belief in witchcraft was rife, not everyone faced with an illness that they did not understand immediately ascribed it to bewitchment; however, many others claimed it was. When young Faith Corbet, the daughter of Henry Corbet of Burton Agnes in the East Riding, fell ill and declared she was bewitched by Alice Huson and Doll Bilby, her mother dismissed such a notion. She had scolded her daughter on a previous occasion for calling Alice an old witch. She liked Alice, a widow, and was kind and generous to her, giving her jobs about the house. She did her best to make the old woman's life easier. Faith, however, hated the old woman and persisted in denouncing her as a witch. When she lost a pair of gloves she swore that Alice had taken them to use in a spell against her and declared that she would never be well again. She then began to suffer from an illness that took the form of violent fits in which she thrashed around shrieking and crying. She needed two or three people to hold her to prevent her biting and scratching anyone and anything she could grasp and, all the time, she was crying, 'Ah, Alice old witch, have I gotten thee!' At other times she lay curled up in her bed, speechless and not eating for days on end, before going to the other extreme of wild behaviour and excessive merriment. Still her parents refused to believe that Alice or witchcraft were involved, and instead sought the advice of doctors from the nearby towns of York, Beverley and Hull. These doctors examined her and questioned her, but each in turn had to admit that he was unable to say what ailed her or to offer any remedy. Her father took her here and there, and sent her for a while to stay with relatives at Pickering, thinking that a change might do her good, but all was to no avail. Faith insisted that she would never be cured as long as Alice Huson and Doll Bilby were free but still her parents resisted the idea of bewitchment. During one of her fits, when a crowd of people came to see her and stood around her bed, Faith called them 'faithless and incredulous people', and asked if they would never believe her until she was dead.

She declared herself already near to death and warned them that, when it was too late, they would be sorry that they had done nothing. This moved her father to go to see Mr Wellfet, the minister of Burton Agnes. Wellfet in turn went to Sir Francis Boynton, the Justice of the Peace. Meanwhile, Mr Corbet dragged Alice Huson into his daughter's bedroom, presumably hoping that, when face to face with Alice, Faith would give up her conviction that she was bewitched. Or perhaps that Alice would be persuaded to confess to witchcraft and remove the spell. Faith gave a terrible shriek when Alice first came into the room but then, after the woman had left, she called for food and drinks and ate and drank heartily. After that, although she had previously seemed too weak to move, even to turn over in her bed, she got up, dressed herself and went downstairs. This was taken by everyone as proof that Alice had some unholy power over her. Although she later had a relapse, when Alice and Doll Bilby were finally arrested and held in secure confinement, Faith declared herself cured and from then on had no more problems.

Alice sealed her fate by confessing to Mr Wellfet, the minister, that she had met with the Devil on the moors and he had promised her that she would want for nothing if she would follow his ways. He appeared, she said, 'like a Black man upon a Black horse, with Cloven Feet; and then I fell down, and did Worship him upon my Knees'. He then gave her five shillings to bind her to him. Another time he gave her seven shillings and repeated the gift on several occasions. She added that she had a witch-mark in the form of a teat, which the Devil sucked on throughout the night, and had done so for the three years since she first met him on the moors. She told Mr Wellfet that when he had questioned her originally the Devil had stood beside her and told her what to say. He had told her not to tell of Doll Bilby, but this time she did implicate Doll. Doll, according to Alice, had wanted to kill Faith outright but Alice had intervened and had only hurt her. She confessed that she had indeed 'ridden' Faith, and that she had decided to practice her witchcraft on the family four years ago when she had gone to beg old clothes from Mrs Corbet but had been refused by the children. She went on to confess to having killed one Dick Warmers with her 'wicked heart and wicked eyes', though she had not been accused of it. Rather less dramatically, she also said that she had lent eight shillings of the Devil's money to a man named Lancelot Harrison. She even confessed to appearing as a black cat at the Corbets' window. By now, Mrs Corbet had finally succumbed to the idea that Alice was a witch and said that she had seen her in this guise looking through the window.

Mr Wellfet duly reported the result of his examinations to Sir Francis Boynton, the Justice of the Peace. As a result of all this outpouring of guilt, Alice Huson and Doll Bilby were both committed to the Assizes at York and sentenced to be hanged. We are left to wonder how a woman could confess to such a tale. Could she really believe that she was a witch and that all she said was true? Or was she an old woman, perhaps grown feeble of mind, who was 'brainwashed' into accepting the suggestions of another person? And what of Faith? Was she play-acting out of malicious dislike? Did she suffer from some hysterical illness, or did she really believe that she was bewitched? It seems strange that a daughter could remain uninfluenced in her beliefs by parents who could resist the idea of witchcraft for as long as four years. But we shall, of course, never know the full truth.

Thomas Jefferson, Mary Jefferson, Margaret Butler and Anon

Woodhouse today is a residential suburb of the south-eastern part of Sheffield. Its humble beginnings were as a farming community, which, with the arrival of coal mining, became a pit village. Coal mining diminished and finally ceased and Woodhouse was overtaken by Sheffield. The only reminders of its ancient past are the stocks and the base of the old market cross, which can still be seen in the centre of the suburb. Its old cottages and a wattle-and-daub building dating from the fifteenth century were demolished in the 1960s.

In 1657, the peaceful rural tenor of Woodhouse was broken by an accusation of witchcraft against four of its inhabitants. Thomas Jefferson, a labourer, was brought to the Assizes on the charge that he had 'entered evil spirits and took up divers dead men, women and children out of their graves, and bewitched Mary Almond of Woodhouse'. Whether this means that Jefferson had actually disturbed the bodies in their graves, or simply that he was thought to have made contact with their spirits, is not clear. It was not unknown for those who believed themselves to have magic powers actually to exhume bodies in order to use the bones in their spells. In 1637, for example, Janet Burniston of Kirby Malzeard near Ripon was accused of taking a skull from a grave to use in a spell to put someone to sleep.

Mary Almond was said to have been 'wasted' by Thomas Jefferson's bewitching, which presumably indicates that she was made ill and incapacitated, but that she had not died. Had the latter been the case, Jefferson, who was found guilty, would surely have been sentenced to hang. As it was he was bound over on 22 March 1658 but freed 'by proclamations' on 26 July. His wife Mary was also charged at the Assizes of a similar offence in November 1657, of entertaining evil spirits and bewitching Beatrice Wynne, who like Mary Almond was declared to have been 'wasted'. Mary was sentenced to be hanged, so it would seem that Beatrice Wynne must have died. The law stated that witchcraft causing death was punishable by hanging and the confiscation of all property. Mary Jefferson, as the wife of a labourer, had no property for the Law to seize, and despite the verdict and sentence, she was granted a reprieve on 22 March 1658 and presumably freed.

The third member of the Woodhouse community to be accused was a widow by the name of Margaret Butler. The charge against her was that she had also been involved with evil spirits and the bewitching of Mary Almond on 2 January 1658. The judgement against her was that she should be hanged, so perhaps at this time Mary Almond did indeed die. There is no record of the sentence being carried out in this case, but neither is she shown to have been reprieved. However, since the others involved were reprieved it seems very likely that she too escaped hanging. We have no name for the fourth person who was charged with the same offence as the other three, but the woman she was said to have bewitched was one Isabel Fidler. The judgement in this case was also that she be hanged but again a reprieve was granted on 22 March 1658.

A contemporary pamphlet published in 1658, a copy of which is in the Bodleian Library, describes the bewitching of two young women, and although it is not expressly stated it is highly probable that it refers to the cases of Mary Jefferson and Margaret Butler. The two bewitched victims were said to have suffered strange fits in which they vomited such objects as pins and wood and the handles of knives, one of which was made of marble. It goes on to state that the evidence did not completely satisfy the judges who 'gave some respite for a more deliberate determination'. If this was indeed a reference to the Woodhouse cases it would offer an explanation for the subsequent reprieves. It was through pamphlets such as this that information and ideas about witchcraft were disseminated, and expectations of what constituted bewitchment were spread.

Joan Jurdie, 1605

Joan Jurdie, the wife of Leonard Jurdie of Rossington near Doncaster, was accused in the spring of 1605 of witchcraft and of causing the death of the wife of Peter Murfin. Joan was accepted as a witch by the villagers, who made use of her supposed powers when it suited them. After the death of Jennet Murfin, the whole village turned against her, and villagers were even prepared to testify to having sought her help in various matters, as evidence against her.

In November 1604, Joan was 'bidden to the labour' of Peter Murfin's wife, but for whatever reason, whether deliberate or unavoidable, she did not turn up until three or four days after the baby was born. Then, adding further insult, she refused to partake of the traditional drink and 'labour-cake' provided. The reason she gave for this unacceptable behaviour was that Peter Murfin did not come into the house to drink with her. The feeling was that she had some ill intent towards the family. Mother and baby had seemed to be doing well and making good progress after the birth, but they began to decline and died two days following Joan's visit. Suspicion gave way to certainty and accusations were made.

Early in the New Year, depositions were made before Hugh Childers, the mayor of Doncaster. Anne Judd, the sister of Jennet Murfin, appeared before him on 6 February, and testified to Joan's behaviour on visiting Jennet. Also she stated that Joan had remarked on leaving that, though Peter Murfin had not come in to drink with her, 'he had as good as have come', which appeared to be a vague threat. Anne Judd went on to add that the next day she had occasion to go to the Jurdies' house, where their servant enquired how her sister and the baby were. Joan Jurdie was also present and, after Anne replied that they were very weak, Joan added that 'she is not at the worst, she will be worse yett'.

On further examination, Anne told how on the night of 15 November Jennet had asked Anne, who was sitting with her, if she was asleep. When she had answered that she was not, Jennet had complained that she was 'ridden with a witch'. A few days later, on the Monday or Tuesday, she told Katherine Dolfin, the wife of William Dolfin, in Anne's hearing that 'She hath kild me. I mone never recover.' When asked who she had in mind, Jennet simply said that she did well until Joan Jurdie came.

Katherine Dolfin, when called before the mayor, confirmed what had been stated by Anne Judd. She said that she had visited Jennet Murfin on Tuesday 18 November and that Jennet had told her, 'I was never well since Satturday that Jurdie wife was here, for the same night I was ridden with a witch, and therefore I could never eate any meate since but suppinge meate.' When asked if she believed that Joan Jurdie was one of those people who could help the bewitched, Katherine replied that she did. She herself, six years before, had been advised to seek her help when her child was sick, and had done so. She had been told to go home, put the child in its cradle and it would presently be well. She testified that she was not alone in her belief that Joan Jurdie could help anything or anybody that was bewitched.

Later that spring, Katherine Dolfin was examined once again before Hugh Childers, Sir John Ferne, the Recorder, and John Carlill, Alderman – three Justices of the Peace. She swore that her former testimony was all true, but added that, when Joan Jurdie had given her help with her sick child, she had told her not to tell anyone lest they thought she was a witch. She reiterated her belief that Jurdie was a witch because one Jane Spight of Rossington had told her she had sought help once for a sick calf. She went on to add that, after her previous examination, Joan Jurdie had threatened both her and her husband. Within a fortnight an ox had fallen sick and three weeks later both a steer and a cow had also gone down with some mysterious illness. None of her neighbours' cattle had fallen sick, only the ones belonging to the Dolfins.

Joan Jurdie herself was then brought before the three Justices of the Peace for examination. She denied all the accusations against her, saying she had no special skills in curing or causing sickness and would never attempt to do so. She had never said Jennet Murfin would be worse when she was sick, nor had she threatened Katherine Dolfin and her husband.

The Jurdies' servant gave evidence that her mistress had given Anne Judd sage leaves and honey to rub on her sister's baby's sore mouth when she called on her. She confirmed also that she did make the remark about Jennet being worse before being better. Jane Spight also gave testimony against Joan with a tale of rumoured threats followed by the sudden death of two of her husband's animals. All these depositions were given by women. None of the husbands appear to have been involved. Even Peter Murfin seems to have stood somewhat aloof from all this, simply testifying that his wife 'within two days after Joan Jurdie had been with her, lyeine in childbed, she dyed, herself growinge sycke immediatelie after her milke turned into bloude'.

Peter Murfin's evidence introduces a slight confusion and inconsistency into the testimonies. Joan was 'bidden to the labour' in November 1604 but did not turn up until the Saturday 15 November. Peter declared that Jennet died two days after

Joan's visit, which would mean that she had died on the Monday. Yet Katherine Dolfin stated that she visited her on Tuesday 18 November with no suggestion that she was visiting a dying woman. This small discrepancy may well have been due to faulty memory, as depositions were being taken in the following year, several months after the death. It could have even have been a mistake by the clerk taking down the testimonies. It does not appear to have been queried or remarked upon. Despite all they were told, the authorities appear to have been convinced by Joan's denials and to have cleared her of any wrongdoing. There is no record of her receiving any punishment.

However, it would seem that the villagers of Rossington retained their hostility towards her. A different source records that she was indicted in 1608 for witchcraft and sorcery that resulted in the deaths of Hester Dolfin, Jane Dolfin, the daughter of William Dolfin, and George Murfin, the son of Peter Murfin. We have no details of these deaths nor of the outcome of the case but, if Joan on this occasion was found guilty, she would certainly have been condemned to hang. It was all a sorry saga to unfold from what seemingly began as offence taken to a slight, on the part of both Joan Jurdie and the villagers of Rossington.

Old Kathy, 1775–1800s

The village of Ruswarp near Whitby, on the North Yorkshire coast, is today a popular tourist spot. A paved way of 1½ miles between Whitby and Ruswarp, known as the Monks' Trod, suggests a past connection of the village with Whitby Abbey. It now provides a pleasant walk for seaside visitors to enjoy boating and canoeing on the River Esk, the miniature railway and the other attractions that Ruswarp has to offer.

During the years between 1775 and the early 1800s, the villagers of Ruswarp lived in terror of Old Kathy, the witch who lived among them. It was dangerous for her to even catch sight of you. If she was out and about everyone made sure to keep out of her way. She was known to have a whole retinue of demons and familiars that she could call up to attack you if you displeased her. And who was to know what might or might not displease her? It was much better just to retreat indoors and avoid the possibility. No one ever called on her and no one had ever seen the inside of her cottage, except for one man, and he was not a Ruswarp villager.

Abe Rogers was a pedlar who travelled around the countryside selling small household goods such as needles and thread, ribbons and even spices to the village wives and farmers' wives. The story told was that Abe met Kathy on the moors one day and they fell into an argument. What it was about no one knows, but it became so heated that Kathy produced a knife and tried to stab Abe. He pushed her to the ground, knocking the knife out of her hand and threatened to strangle her. Kathy screamed out some strange magic words and called up her demons. They advanced and surrounded Abe but he was not afraid. Quickly taking a pinch of some substance from his pack, he flung it into the air towards them, causing a blinding dust. While Kathy and the creatures could not see he took up the knife and struck out at them before making his escape. He injured some of the creatures, but oddly, although it was widely believed that any injury to a witch's familiars caused similar suffering to the witch, Kathy was unscathed.

Such a story seems a strange basis for a friendship, yet ever afterwards Abe Rogers visited Old Kathy in her cottage whenever his travels took him to Ruswarp. Could the reality be that Old Kathy was simply a naturally bad-tempered old woman who had been made more ill-natured and crotchety by the villagers' attitude to her? A case of 'give a dog a bad name'... Perhaps when Abe met Kathy on the moors, they had an amicable and friendly conversation and Kathy invited him to visit her, glad to entertain someone who saw her simply as an old and lonely woman. The villagers, with their preconceived idea of Kathy, found such a friendship impossible to grasp and had to construct what was to them a more plausible reason. Namely, that Abe was himself something of a witch and his magic more powerful than Kathy's.

There is a doll still in Whitby Museum, which is said to be Kathy and to be the only likeness of a North Yorkshire witch that represents an actual individual. Certainly the doll shows Kathy to be the typical stereotype of a witch in appearance. And as we have seen, that alone was often sufficient for some poor old woman to be regarded with fear and named as a witch. The people of Ruswarp continued to fear Old Kathy and remembered her long after she was dead.

Old Kathy of Ruswarp doll in the Whitby Museum. (*Reproduced with the permission of the Whitby Literary & Philosophical Society*)

Old Sally Kindreth, 1800–1810

Belief in witchcraft lingered on a long time in rural areas, and Sally Kindreth of Scorton near Richmond in North Yorkshire was reputed to be active between 1800 and 1810 when she went to live with a niece in Lancashire. Old Sally was crippled as a young girl when a beam fell on her. It severely injured her back, which became permanently twisted. As a result of this she was regularly taunted and tormented, and even physically assaulted by unkind youths in the village.

On one such occasion they had dragged her down to the water's edge, and were struggling with her with the intention of throwing her into the River Swale, when a passing stranger came to her rescue. He told the youths to leave her alone and said that he would fight whoever was willing among the group if they let go of Old Sally. Being cowards, none among them seemed very keen, but finally George Pennock agreed to accept the challenge, only to be thoroughly beaten. George was a good-looking lad and cocky with it, and because of that he was allowed to take the role of leader as long as things were going well for the group. When he was beaten his comrades deserted him, as is so often the case.

Old Sally, who had a reputation for cursing and casting spells on those she disliked was not going to let this opportunity pass and cursed him roundly. 'There are more seeds in a poppy-head than there are days left for him,' she is supposed to have said. 'He'll die with his head under water but he won't die of drowning.' George may have recovered his cockiness and felt that he could dismiss the enigmatic threat of an old crone but he would have done better to have mended his wicked ways. Old Sally's words were to come true within a very short time.

Not long after the incident involving George and Old Sally it happened that a young married couple, Tom and Polly Kaye, failed to return when expected from Bolton-on-Swale where they had been visiting Polly's mother. After a while their friends and neighbours became very anxious and feared that something must have happened to them. They decided to consult William Boddy, the cobbler, who had a reputation as a wise man. William also had a magic glass in which he could see things as if they were projected on a screen. It was said to be a piece of glass from one of the nearby Abbeys, saved from the time of the Dissolution. They hoped that this very special glass would tell them where to find Tom and Polly. William duly looked in his glass where he saw a terrible sight. Polly and Tom were to be seen walking home along the banks of the Swale and George Pennock was there creeping up behind them. He hit Tom on the head and abducted Polly. Aghast at this news a search-party immediately set out and discovered Tom lying unconscious on the river bank but there was no sign of Polly and no clue as to where she might have been taken.

It was now Old Sally's turn to take a hand in events. She was asked to help in finding Polly. To do so she took some coins that Polly had handled and covered them with quicksilver before pushing them into a loaf of bread. This was thrown into the Swale at the point where Tom had been found. As it floated downstream they followed it until it came to rest by the bank, and Polly's body was found nearby. A warrant was issued for the arrest of George Pennock but he was nowhere to be found. Tom recovered from his injuries and swore that he would never rest until he found George Pennock and had justice for the assault and murder of his wife. Wherever he went in his job as a waggoner he continued his search. Old Sally insisted that he would never catch him, but he would be found at the end of fifteen months.

And so it turned out. One night in October of the following year, Tom and a group of waggoners were sitting in the comfort of the Salutation Inn at Leeming, sheltering from a terrible storm. Amidst the noise of the wind and the storm they suddenly heard a most terrible sound like the yelping of several dogs. It was Gabriel's Hounds they said, a sure sign of a death and they felt a cold icy shiver run up their backs. After a while a frightened stable lad came rushing in to tell them that there was a body lying face down in the horse-trough outside. When the body was carried into the inn Tom saw that it was George Pennock. He had been stabbed in the back and had toppled face-down into the trough. Old Sally's words had come true. He had certainly died with his head underwater but not of drowning.

Tom Kaye rejoiced that Pennock had paid for the murder of his wife, but was glad that he had not found him as he would surely then have become a murderer himself. George Pennock's murderer was never found. So was it pure coincidence that Sally Kindreth's words came true or should we believe in her curse? Common sense says not, but who knows …

Jane Kighly, 1649

The supposed power of a witch to cause harm with speed and effectiveness by such simple means as a mere touch must have been a cause of great fear to those who believed it. In 1649, a man named Abraham Hobson of Idle near Bradford claimed that Jane Kighly came into his house and stroked his pig, which was by the fire, declaring that it would go mad and die. This it did within half an hour. It is a well-known practice of farmers and others to bring small sick animals in to the warmth of the fire, and so one cannot but wonder if the pig was already sick and dying before Jane, perhaps recognising the signs, possibly stroked it sympathetically.

However, Mr Hobson went on to declare that at a 'pig feast', which he attended, Jane who was also present told him that she loved him and clapped him on the knee. The next day the knee was inflamed and eventually became paralysed. The touch did not need to be a blow. In another recorded case, a Mary Allanson of Appleton Wiske near Northallerton in North Yorkshire became ill a mere hour after Elizabeth Lively had taken her hand and thanked her for the alms she was given.

Elizabeth Lambe, 1653

Although many people were very much afraid of witches and their power to cause harm, it would seem that not everybody was. There were those who were not afraid to confront the witch they believed had harmed them and, indeed, were prepared to attack her. They may have been simply bent on punishment and revenge, or intent on drawing blood in the generally held belief that to do so would cause the witch to lose her power over them.

A case from Reedness, which lies near Goole on the southern bank of the Ouse just before it joins the River Humber, demonstrates both these possibilities. On 17 March 1653, John Johnson of Reedness accused Elizabeth Lambe before William Adams, presumably the local magistrate. She had appeared, he said, at night by his bedside accompanied by an old man in brown clothing on several occasions. He had been 'very much affrighted but had not power to speak to her'. He did not say who the old man with Elizabeth was and perhaps he did not know. The description of the gentleman as dressed in brown may have had some significance then but, if so, it is lost on us today. John Johnson went on to say that, after the first time this happened, his stock fell sick and no one was able to tell him what it was they were suffering from. He heard that others among his neighbours had the same problem with stock that was ill or dying, and they put this down to bewitchment by Elizabeth Lambe. He said 'that they also did beat her and was never afterwards disquieted by her'. This somewhat ambiguous phrase could be taken to imply that he too had beaten her. Nicholas Baldwin, also of Reedness, testified that in 1648 Elizabeth Lambe had by her witchcraft caused three of his foals to die at birth. He then confessed that he had taken his stick and beaten her, and had his wife not gone down on her knees and begged him to stop and forgive her he would have beaten her still worse. This suggests a very severe beating to have caused his wife to plead on Elizabeth's behalf.

Thomas Rennerd, the constable of Reedness, said that his child was ill in 1651 and his wife believed that Elizabeth Lambe was responsible. Not long afterwards she met Elizabeth who went down on her knees and asked for forgiveness, after which the child recovered. In the case of illness due to bewitchment it was believed that if the witch could be induced to ask her victim to forgive her the illness would be cured. Since this was tantamount to admitting that one was a witch and guilty of bewitchment it was never an easy thing to obtain from those accused. Mrs Rennerd must have been very persuasive.

Finally, John Wreight gave witness that he had been with Richard Browne of Reedness when he was ill and Browne said that 'he was cruelly handled at the heart' with Elizabeth Lambe and that she 'drew his heart's blood from him'. He asked John to bring Elizabeth to his house so that he might scratch her and draw her blood as she had drawn his, and so be cured. By means of a trick Elizabeth was brought to the house and Richard Browne asked her why she had done this to him. He said if she hurt him no more he would forgive her. Elizabeth made no reply and Richard scratched her until she bled. Despite this he died a week later, complaining all the time to John Wreight that, if he died, Elizabeth Lambe had killed him.

There seems to be no record of any punishment of Elizabeth Lambe so she may have been acquitted. But we may well feel that she had already suffered enough from the several beatings she had received.

Male Witches and Wise Men

Although it was more usual for women to practise the supernatural arts of witchcraft it was by no means unknown for men also to do so. As early as 1286, Godfrey Darel, a Cistercian monk at Rievaulx Abbey, was reported to the Archbishop of York for practising the Dark Arts. In 1571 a Peter Carter was charged in York together with Edward More, a relative of Sir Thomas More – the statesman and Lord Chancellor who was executed in 1535 for refusing to recognise Henry VIII as Head of the Church. The case against Peter Carter was dismissed and Edward More was given a penance, but the following year a man named Roger Wyerthorne was hanged at York for witchcraft. Robert Conyers, a gentleman of the upper class from Guisborough, was fined at Helmsley in 1657 for wickedly practising 'certain detestable arts of sorcery'. We do not know exactly what he was said to have done. However, he was a gentleman of means and he may well have been ahead of his times. He may have been engaged in scientific experimentation, a hobby bound to cause suspicion at a time of ignorance when even educated men believed in witchcraft.

In 1606 Ralph Milner, a yeoman landowner of Muker, appeared at the Richmond Quarter Sessions accused of 'sorcery, witchcraft, enchantment, and telling of fortunes'. He was ordered to 'make his submission at Mewcarr (Muker) Church upon Sunday next in time of Divine Service and confess that he hath highly offended God and deluded man and is heartily sorry and will offend no more'. This may seem a remarkably light punishment for the time but it was no more so than many others in the North Riding. Those who sought the advice of these sorcerers, or 'wise men' as they were known, were also liable to be brought before the authorities, as Thomas Robinson of Kirkby Grindalyth in the East Riding discovered in 1688 when he consulted one about a health problem.

Most communities had their wise man or wise woman to whom they turned for help with their problems. With ignorance and superstition abounding, no vets, and doctors whose idea of treatment often involved merely 'bleeding', it was inevitable that people sought out anyone who professed to be able to help them. Wise men (or women) often had knowledge of herbs and natural remedies, but they also claimed to tell fortunes, to find lost or stolen property and to break spells cast by witches. Some genuinely used their powers, whether herbal skills or psychological methods, for the good of their clients rather than for evil purposes; others simply took advantage of people's ignorance and gullibility for their own gain. The women were often still given the title of witch. The men were generally known as wise men or occasionally 'Cunning-men'.

After 1736, witchcraft was no longer a capital offence and was accepted as more a crime of deception and delusion than the practice of magic powers. The wise man became more open in offering his services, and we know, for example, that in 1773 Master Sadler of Bedale in the Dales advertised his services for the cure of the 'ague'. This he declared would be achieved by reciting an incantation whilst writing the patient's name on the back of his fireplace! His services together with another Bedale wise man were called for in the case of the witch Molly Cass, who caused a great deal of trouble in the area.

John Wrightson, the wise man of Stokesley, also advertised his services, making much of his being the seventh son of a seventh son, a fact which was generally believed to convey special powers. In 1808, he had a Whitby firm publish the following notice: 'The seventh son John Wrightson begs leave to acquaint the public that those who are afflicted with any kind of inward disorder, white swellings, scurvy, or any kind of shortness of breath may be relieved by sending him their water. (Likewise cattle that do not thrive).' He was a curer of cattle by profession and undoubtedly possessed knowledge and skills in that direction. Lacking anyone else to turn to, people not unnaturally began to ask for his help with their own problems. He was not about to turn away what could be a profitable sideline for him and went on to actively encourage the idea.

Wrightson was not content, however, to confine himself to dealing with ailments in which he had some expertise. He also undertook to deal with cases of supposed bewitchment. He appeared to know a person's background and what it was they wished to consult him about before they actually told him. How he managed this uncanny achievement we do not know but he gained a reputation as a result for what seemed like extraordinary magical powers. He embellished his image by wearing a cloak and pointed hat in consultations. People brought him their problems from considerable distances away. He was involved in curing one of Nanny Pierson's victims in Goathland, which is quite a long way for someone to travel to Stokesley in order to seek his advice. His fame had clearly spread across North Yorkshire. Eventually, for some reason, Wrightson was accused of fraud. He fled to Malton but, in 1818, he was charged there with assault. Whilst travelling to his trial at Northallerton Quarter Sessions, he committed suicide by taking poison in the coach he was being moved in as it passed through the village of Ampleforth.

Mark Jopling, a weaver of Brompton near Northallerton, had valuable cloth and tools stolen from his workshop sometime in the early nineteenth century. It was natural that he should consult a wise man. Helping to locate lost or stolen property was a service regularly offered by them. And so, since Mark Jopling was

Splintwork in Whitby museum
used by a wise man in casting
spells. (*Reproduced with the
permission of the Whitby Literary
& Philosophical Society*)

too busy with his work and sorting out his workshop after the break-in, two of his friends went to consult the wise man of Sowerby on his behalf. This wise man had a special piece of equipment, a crystal ball about the size of a goose egg. The two friends were told to look into it and see what it might tell them about the robbery. As they were instructed they each in turn gazed earnestly at the crystal but could see nothing. 'Ah,' said the wise man. 'Obviously you were not born under the right planet.' However, by great good fortune, he knew of a lad who was, and this lad was sent for to look in the crystal. He was apparently able to see the thieves in Mark Jopling's workshop and to follow them in their flight to Yarm and then on to Thornaby-on-Tees where they booked into an inn. Even more miraculously he could hear them planning to leave the following morning at 8.00 a.m. Intent on catching the thieves, Jopling's two friends hurriedly paid the lad and sped off on horseback. They made the journey in record time only to find on arrival that they had a serious problem. Thornaby-on-Tees had three public houses and the lad had failed to tell them the name of the one into which the thieves had booked. With only a vague description of the men they wanted, they tried all three pubs, but perhaps unsurprisingly they were unsuccessful.

Jonathan Westcott (or Westwick as he was also known) of Upleatham, was a gamekeeper but he was also much in demand in his other capacity as the local wise man. It was to him that the local people turned for help when things occurred that they could not account for. Peggy Flounders, the Marske witch, provided Jonathan with many opportunities to demonstrate his skills by remedying the nasty things that happened to the people she was believed to have bewitched.

George Wales (1786–1860) of Barmby in the East Riding was particularly well known for his exorcisms of evil spirits and witches and also for his help in finding stolen property. He was a keen astronomer and his wanderings around the countryside at night in pursuit of this interest caused much speculation that he was in contact with the powers of darkness. On one occasion he visited a farm where many cattle had unaccountably fallen sick or died. He promised to lift the curse that was supposed to have been laid upon it. This he did by having the young foal that was the most recent death buried in a deep pit in the road into the stockyard. He then ordered horseshoes to be nailed above the doors of the stable and recited an incantation from the book of charms that he possessed. It was the book from which he also took the words for his exorcism rite. A staunchly religious man, he always began by calling on the power of God and Jesus Christ and followed it by the words:

I exorcise and conjure thee, thou fearful and accursed spirit, by the holy and wonderful names of the Almighty Jehovah ... I exorcise and conjure, I invoke and command thee thou aforesaid spirit by the power of angels, archangels Cherubim and Seraphim ... by the blood of Abel, by the righteousness of Seth and the prayers of Noah, by the voices of thunder and by the dreadful day of judgement by all those powerful and royal words aforesaid, that, without delay or malicious intent thou do quit this daughter of Adam and torment her no more forever. These things I command thee in the power of Him who hath sanctified the name of the Father, the Son and the Holy Ghost. Amen.

With slight amendments to fit the person involved and spoken in a voice of sonorous authority, it must surely have had a chilling and awe-inspiring effect on all who heard it. What evil spirit could possibly withstand such a powerful command!

Known only by his initials, J. S. of Haisthorpe was another wise man active in the East Riding around the year 1840. His story was recorded by a Dr R. Wood of Driffield. The speciality of J. S. was what he termed 'faith-healing' and he appears to have practised it with remarkable success. In the case of a woman from Holderness who became ill and lost the use of her legs, he diagnosed bewitchment. With his magical powers he was able to discover the witch and declared that she would die and the woman would then recover. The alleged witch did indeed soon die and the woman was able to walk again. Another woman from Speeton who had been bedridden for years was cured by J. S. The grateful woman and her friends are said to have celebrated on three successive Sundays, praising God and singing hymns and dancing through the streets of Bridlington.

A man in Kirkburn also had cause to be grateful for the services of J. S. He had been unwell for some time and had lost cattle and his favourite old mare. But things finally came to a head when, one Saturday evening, he and his wife were sitting comfortably and companionably by the fire. The clock began suddenly to make strange moaning sounds. The man suspected that a certain woman had bewitched him and J. S. was sent for. He arrived by carrier's cart and at midnight he began the ceremony to free the man and his wife from the witch's power. A reading from the Bible was followed by the Lord's Prayer said backwards. Next the heart of a black hen was torn out and stuck with pins before being buried in the garden. Finally a 'fizzing stuff' had water poured on it while several incantations were made. The substance boiled and bubbled and gave off such fumes that the man and his wife fled back into the house in alarm, to be troubled no more. The carrier apparently had been somewhat sceptical of the wise man's powers but was not prepared to test them further when J. S. offered to call up the Devil on the way home. 'I have tried to keep him off me all my life,' the carrier said, 'and I do not want to see him now.'

It is interesting that, although we may consider the wise men to be largely tricksters, particularly in their claims to be able to cast off bewitchment, nonetheless they all seemed to work to a similar pattern. They were not, it seems, just 'making it up as they went along'. All seemed to have some element of religion, ceremonies at midnight, the heart of a hen of a specific colour, or other creature, with pins stuck in it before burial, special ingredients causing fumes, and mysterious chants. We know that George Wales had his book of charms. Was there perhaps a common handbook of instructions that they all worked from?

Margaret Morton, 1650

On 10 January 1650, Joan Booth, wife of William Booth of Warmefield in the West Riding, stood before four Justices of the Peace under the chairmanship of Sir John Savile, in Wakefield to accuse Margaret Morton of Kirkthorpe of witchcraft. She stated that Margaret Morton came to her house one day and gave her four-year-old son a piece of bread; an innocent, even kindly thing to do, one might think. But Margaret had been suspected for many years of being a witch, as had her mother and sister, now both dead. And so, when Joan's son became mysteriously ill, having previously been a well and happy, sturdy little boy, it was natural that her thoughts and fears turned to bewitchment. It was an accepted fact that witches could bewitch by as little as a casual touch, or by giving or taking something from their victim. When Joan remembered the giving of that piece of bread, it was inevitable that her suspicion should fall on Margaret. She described to the Justices how her son became sick and how his body first swelled up to an unusual size before gradually weakening and wasting away. He became so weak that eventually he could neither walk nor stand.

Joan then sent for Margaret who came to the house and was prevailed upon to ask forgiveness of the child, which she did three times. Although this was as good as confessing that she was a witch she seemed quite willing to do so. She also offered no resistance to being pricked with a pin to draw blood. Both these actions were recognised means of removing a spell and appear to have worked successfully. According to Joan's statement, her son immediately became better. Yet despite this she still went ahead with her accusation of Margaret. She then remembered all the times that she had been unsuccessful in churning her butter and making her cheese, and decided with hindsight that these too were the fault of Margaret Morton's witchcraft. They were added to her deposition.

Next Frances Ward, wife of John Ward of Kirkthorpe, gave evidence of Margaret's reputation as a witch. Frances stated that two years previously two of her children had died after being very ill. Margaret Morton had been in the room when one of them died, and the child had said, 'Good mother, put out Morton.' Not, one would have thought, a very convincing proof of witchcraft! Mrs Ward had then gone on to say that she was one of the four women ordered to search Margaret for the 'witch mark'. When they had done so, they had found two black spots between her thigh and her body. They were raised like warts but were not warts. One was black on both sides, an inch wide and blue in the middle. Very dark moles can often appear black and blueish and be raised like warts, but whatever these blemishes were they may well have been strange and unknown to the searchers. Despite this very thin case against her, Margaret Morton was tried at the Assizes. Not surprisingly, given the quality of the evidence, she was acquitted.

Old Nanny of Great Ayton

Towards the end of the nineteenth century, Richard Blakeborough collected stories of North Riding witches, interviewing and questioning older men and women who had first-hand knowledge and experience of witches in their youth. He included what he had learned in his book *Yorkshire Wit, Character, Folklore and Customs*, published in 1898. He also wrote a dramatic narrative poem, 'The Hunt of Yatton Brig', which tells a story about the witch known as Old Nanny. Yatton is the local name for Great Ayton, which is where Nanny lived. She had a cottage at a corner of the green near the mill and terrorized the villagers among others far and wide.

Johnny Simpson of Newton-under-Roseberry called on Nanny one day seeking revenge after being jilted by his girlfriend, Mary. She was about to marry Tom Smith and Johnny wanted Nanny's help in spoiling the couple's happy day. Nanny was willing to oblige and suggested things that she might do. She could cause them both to go blind, she could strike Tom with a hideous disfigurement or she could even cause them to part for ever. All this was too drastic for Johnny. What he had intended was more in the way of relatively trivial matters going wrong, such as the ring being dropped, things happening that were considered unlucky omens, or perhaps an argument on the wedding night. If Nanny could do that for him he swore he would be her friend for life. Nanny was scornful and told him that she reckoned nothing to anything he might swear. What he wanted done he would have to do for himself she said. She gave him instructions as to what he should do to achieve what he wanted. He was to go to Ayton Bridge, wave Nanny's broom three times above his head, go backwards into the churchyard and collect some soil there. Then he was to wash his hands in the old well and leave Nanny's broom beside it for her to collect.

Johnny carried out the first part of his instructions all right but gave up before he washed his hands and threw Nanny's broom aside into the beck. When he set off home he was followed by a huge crowd of frightful creatures, huge bats and owls and even skeletons. Then at the bridge he met three 'night hags' who screamed that he was in their power because he had disobeyed Nanny and misused her broom. They told him he would be hunted by them and their familiars with the words:

> We've owlets trained
> A clutch of bats
> Flay-bogles without feet
> We've goblin dogs
> And great big frogs
> They'll all hunt thee to-neet.

Then they grabbed him and carried him up Roseberry Topping, tossing him between them, turning him and twisting him this way and that throughout the night until he felt almost battered to death. He returned home at last regretting that he had ever been to see Old Nanny. Such was the story that was told to Richard Blakeborough and which inspired him to write his great dialect poem.

Another story of Old Nanny was told to him by the granddaughter of Mary Langstaff who lived in Stokesley, and it concerned Mary and her cousin Martha Sokeld. One day, Martha was taken ill and sent for Mary to come to Kildale to nurse her. Although it was a fair distance away, Mary set off on foot, that being her only option in those days. She had not gone far when she met an old woman that she 'didn't leyke t' leeak on' and felt sure was the old witch. Not wanting to speak to her she turned aside and began to pick the wayside flowers. Old Nanny took exception to being ignored and told Mary so in no uncertain terms, ending with the threat, 'Ah'll paay tha oot for't'. Fortunately Mary was wearing a sprig of rowan, that magical protector against witches, and so Nanny was unable to harm her then. Mary stayed with her cousin until she recovered before returning home to Stokesley.

A few days later she was very surprised when her cousin appeared at her door. She said she had been ill again and thought she was not going to last long. But she wanted to see her sister in Northallerton before she died. If Mary would put her up for the night she would continue her journey by the carrier in the morning. She then asked Mary to go on an errand for her while she rested and urged her not to hurry back as she wouldn't like to be wakened before she had had a good sleep. Mary went but after a while began to have misgivings that she could not explain so turned around and hurried back. She approached very quietly and peeped in through the window. She was amazed to see her cousin dropping things into a pan on the fire and to hear her chanting:

> Fire cum
> Fire gan
> Curling smeeak
> Keep oot o' t' pan

This was followed by a list of gruesome ingredients and ending with the words:

> It boils, thoo'll drink
> He'll speeak, thoo'll think
> It boils, thoo'll see
> He'll speeak , thoo'll dee.

Mary realised at once that this was the witch in the guise of her cousin and felt sure that she was devising a spell to cause harm to her and her sweetheart. She marched fearlessly into the house and confronted her. Holding out the Bible she told her to do her worst but she trusted in the Bible. The witch turned the pan upside-down on the fire, screaming that she would have her revenge on her yet, and disappeared.

The next morning a messenger arrived from Kildale to say that Martha Sokeld had disappeared and had not been seen for several days. Her body was found three days later on the moors. Everyone concluded that Old Nanny had killed her and taken over her appearance in order to harm Mary Langstaff. Whether she made any more attempts we do not know, but we do know that Mary lived to be eighty-five and brought up a large family. If Old Nanny did try she was obviously unsuccessful. But perhaps Mary always wore her sprig of rowan or kept the Bible handy!

One mile east of Great Ayton lies the Nanny Howe Bronze Age burial mound, one of at least three tumuli described in an archaeological survey of 1933 as being associated with a prehistoric settlement. Both tumuli and settlement are now lost to woodland. Tradition says that on a certain night at midnight a once-noted witch named Nanny Howe can be seen astride her broomstick riding over Howe Wood. She was said to have once chased the Devil in this fashion for miles when they had fallen out. This must surely refer to Old Nanny of Great Ayton, who was described by the old people to Richard Blakeborough.

Mary Pannell of Ledston

The village of Ledston on the road built by the Romans between Castleford in West Yorkshire and York seems to have changed little over the centuries. It is not difficult to imagine it as it would be in the distant past. Even Ledston Luck colliery nearby – now no more – made little effect on the village with its old houses and seventeenth-century hall. The road is straight, as roads of Roman origin invariably are, but a short distance from Castleford towards Ledston there is a rise and a small wooded hill named Mary Pannell Hill. To have a street, a place or a feature of the landscape named after one is an honour usually reserved for a national hero, or a local worthy, someone respected in their community. This small hill, however, is remembered as a place of execution, the place where the witch Mary Pannell was burned to death at the very end of the reign of Queen Elizabeth I.

There are as many stories about Mary as there are variations on the spelling of her name. In one she is said to have lived in a hut in the village of Ledston, where she dealt with evil spirits and made potions, curses and spells, which were popularly sought after. Another version says that she was a maid at Ledston Hall, at that time a modest dwelling of monastic origin acquired by the Witham family during the Reformation. When the young master fell ill with a chill, Mary made up a potion for him. By mistake his mother gave it to him orally instead of rubbing it on his chest as was intended. He died and Mary was accused of having bewitched him and killed him with her evil magic. She fled on horseback but her horse went lame and she was overtaken and captured by her pursuers.

Yet another story has it that she was accused by Dame Mary Bolles of Heath Hall near Wakefield of killing her father William Witham by witchcraft. Mary Pannell promptly cursed Dame Mary, causing her to die as well. Since Dame Mary died in 1662 in her eighties, long after Mary Pannell was executed in 1603, her death can certainly not be laid at Mary's door! This would seem to be a case of tales of local history and local legends becoming entwined and muddled over the years. What is certain is that Mary Pannell was accused, tried and executed as a witch.

Since that time, local superstition has it that her ghost, leading a horse, can be seen at Ledston Hall and Mary Pannell Hill, and that this is a sight that is bound to lead to a death in the family of anyone unfortunate enough to see her. Even in modern times, some claim that cars on the road at that point have mysteriously come to a sudden halt for no apparent reason, and misty figures have been seen. Children playing on the wooded hill describe being suddenly overcome with a sense of fear that sends them scurrying home.

Common sense suggests that Mary Pannell was one of those women in the past that had a particular knowledge of herbs and cures. Gladly resorted to by an ignorant populace when the need arose, these women were no longer tolerated when things did not work out well and were often accused of witchcraft.

Nanny Pierson and the 'Witch-Hares' of the North York Moors

The village of Goathland lies high in the North York Moors between Pickering and Whitby. Eleven miles north of Pickering the road branching off the A169 main road to Whitby brings one, after three more miles, to the village. It was once a quiet, peaceful place known only to a few visitors interested in the nearby Roman Road, its several impressive waterfalls, and walking in the beautiful moorland round about; but Goathland is now a busy tourist attraction. After its years as the location for the television series *Heartbeat* and the use of its railway station as 'Hogsmeade station' in the *Harry Potter* films, it is not visited so much for itself but to experience the fictional village of Aidensfield, or in order to arrive on the North York Moors Railway at Hogsmeade Station. Visitors want to feel when they see the place on-screen that they have been there and know it, and indeed may actually have seen the actors involved, in person, as they filmed.

Even in the latter half of the twentieth century it was not unknown for Goathland to be totally cut off by severe winter weather long enough for essential supplies to run out, which then had to be dropped in by helicopter. During the winter snows of 2010, roads were blocked and drivers stranded in their cars on the moors. Imagine then how it must have been in earlier times in such remote areas when roads, if they existed at all, were poor. Places such as Goathland were accessible only by paths and tracks over the moors, known in these parts as 'trods'. Travelling was difficult whatever the weather. Cut off from any great knowledge of the wider world, an isolated village was a breeding ground for superstition and the belief in magic that persisted even when times grew better. There have been people who practised magic and witchcraft from the very beginning of time, and also those who turned to them in ignorance and need for help with their problems. Goathland had Nanny Pierson. She would seem to have been active in the nineteenth century but it is difficult to be certain of her exact dates as Pierson is a very common name in the area. Nanny was not a kindly witch. She had the power to cripple people and she used it, allegedly even on an unborn child.

Gawain Pierson, a farmer at Thornhill Farm, had two daughters, Ann and Mary, one of whom had been confined to bed for three years. No one knew what was wrong with her, but everyone was sure that Nanny was the cause of it. Eventually the local schoolmaster, though sceptical, was persuaded by his friend Gawain to consult the wise man of Stokesley on his behalf. He told the wise man on his arrival that he did not believe in witchcraft and bewitchment. Nevertheless, he was taken aback by the wise man's powers when he said to him, 'Then tha'd better have stayed at home and mended thi window.' A window had been broken just before the schoolmaster left home and the same thought had crossed his mind, though he had not voiced it to anyone. The wise man read an incantation from a large book and suddenly Nanny's face appeared at the window, although Stokesley is a good distance from Goathland. Thus impressed, the schoolmaster swore as requested never to reveal anything seen or heard at the wise man's house and carried out all the instructions he was given. On his return to Goathland he found Gawain Pierson's daughter sitting up in bed. She was obviously on the mend. Nanny's spell had been broken, though no one knew how.

On another occasion, when the Squire's beautiful daughter formed an attachment to a young farmer who was considered an unsuitable suitor, she stubbornly refused to give him up. The Squire had in mind for her a man, old and ugly but with a goodly amount of money. He called on Nanny for help. She, no doubt in return for payment in cash or kind, cast a spell that caused the poor girl to become paralysed and unable to walk. As she lay in her room and day followed day without the young man being able to see his love, he, in his turn, consulted a wise man in Scarborough. He was given a glass into which he was to gaze steadily until he saw the likeness of someone. Presently he said he could see Nanny Pierson and was told that she was at the bottom of his problem. The advice he was given was daunting. He was to obtain blood of the witch, mix it with holy water and the milk from a red cow, apply it to his sweetheart's feet and so remove the spell. Acquiring the milk was easy but he was presented with two problems to overcome: how to obtain the blood and holy water and how to gain access to the girl's room. He refused to give in and finally came up with the answers.

It was a well-known fact that Nanny Pierson often changed herself into a hare, and so the young farmer took his gun and some bullets made of silver – the only kind capable of killing a witch. He watched and waited until he saw Nanny in the form of a hare and then he shot her. Although he only wounded her and she escaped, he was able to collect some blood from the ground. He stole some holy water from the church and with his precious prize he climbed secretly in the night through his sweetheart's bedroom window and applied the potion as he had been told. Immediately the spell was broken and he carried her off, hopefully to live happily ever after. Nanny meanwhile was limping with a sore leg and facing the rage of the Squire.

It was accepted everywhere that witches could change into animal form, the idea of the hare being particularly popular in this area of Yorkshire. There are many similar stories told, though the one involving Nanny Pierson of Goathland is perhaps the best known. The author Peter Walker in his book *Murders and Mysteries from the North York Moors* tells of a Glaisdale witch known as Aud Maggie who, in the form of a hare, was believed to be destroying a nursery of young saplings by eating off the tops. The farmer made bullets from his silver buttons and set off with his shotgun to deal with her. He succeeded only in severely injuring her, but she 'hoppled away as wheel as she could' to Maggie's house. The next day Maggie was found in bed with severe injuries that she claimed were due to a fall on broken glass. A likely story!

Another tale relates to an incident as recently as 1860 and originates apparently from the personal experience of Bobby Dowson who was a famous Bilsdale huntsman. When he died in 1902 the Vicar refused to have his gravestone in the churchyard because it was carved with his hunting gear, and so it was placed outside the Sun Inn, his favourite pub at Bilsdale on the Helmsley to Stokesley road. According to Dowson's story, he and a group of friends were hunting hares when they chased one to the barn of Peg Humphrey of East Moors, near Helmsley. It disappeared through a hole in the door and when they entered the barn they found no hare but Peg panting and breathless lying on the straw. She made an excuse for being breathless and claimed the door had blown shut on her.

On yet another occasion Bobby claimed to have chased a hare that ran to Peg's house after being bitten on the leg by one of the hounds. It ran straight through the wall of the house according to the account. On entering, the hunters found Peg, exhausted and suffering from a leg injury. She was treated by the doctor but was lame for the rest of her life. Nanny, a witch from Westerdale, was unusual in that she seemed to actually enjoy being chased in the form of a hare and would tell the men out hunting where they were sure to raise a hare. On one occasion when she did so she told them on no account must they let loose their black dog on the animal. They found a hare where nanny had suggested and gave chase but did not catch it. Just as they were giving up on it for the day, the black dog rushed after the hare and caught it by the leg before it got away. When the men, full of apologies, called on Nanny they found her, like Peg Humphrey, with a painful wound in her thigh.

All the tales of hare-witches, of which these are but a small sample, follow the same pattern. A long chase but failure to kill or capture, an injury by dog-bite or shotgun, entry by the hare to a house or other premises, followed by discovery of the witch within with similar injuries. The interesting thing about them, beyond the concentration of such stories in this particular area, is the fact that witches were believed in and often feared but were used and tolerated long after the 'witch-craze' of the 1600s. As we have seen, they were in evidence as recently as the late nineteenth century. Indeed, there is even a report of a man just before the Second World War, asking someone for a sixpence to make a silver bullet to kill a witch in the form of a dog that was worrying his sheep.

Jennet Preston, 1612

Jennet Preston is known as one of the Lancashire witches, the famous Pendle witches who were given their name from Pendle Hill near Clitheroe in whose shadow they lived. In fact, she was a Yorkshire woman who lived with her husband, William Preston, at Gisburn, which lies between Clitheroe and Skipton in Yorkshire, very close to the border between the two counties. There have been changes to the borders since 1974 but in those days Gisburn was in the Craven area of Yorkshire. For this reason, when she was accused of witchcraft, she was tried and executed in York and not in Lancaster as the other so-called Pendle witches were.

Thomas Lister, the man she was accused of murdering by witchcraft, was a gentleman of some standing in the West Riding of Yorkshire and the chief landowner in Gisburn. He lived at Westby Hall, the seat of the Lister family until the eighteenth century. Jennet Preston lived nearby. It was a well known fact and widely acknowledged that Jennet was a welcome and frequent presence at the Lister house, and received great kindness and many favours from Thomas Lister. This is clear from the evidence given at her trial but it is not certain what her relationship was with the family. Was she a servant, or a tenant? Or was she, as Jonathan Lumby suggests in his searching and excellent book *The Lancashire Witch Craze*, the mistress of Thomas Lister? We do not know.

In February 1607, Thomas Lister died of a seizure or heart attack, aged only thirty-eight, while attending the wedding of his sixteen-year-old son – who was also called Thomas – to Jane Heber. She was the daughter of the magistrate Thomas Heber, who four years later prosecuted Jennet Preston at the behest of Thomas Lister Junior, a fact that may or may not be significant. As he lay dying Thomas Lister cried out that 'Jennet Preston lays heavie upon me. Preston's wife lays heavie upon me'. He begged those present to find her and not to let her leave the house. Nothing seems to have been made of this at the time, but Thomas Lister, the son, and a woman named Anne Robinson, later testified to this fact at the trial as proof that he was accusing her of having bewitched him. However, as Lumby points out,

Gisburn village today. (*Graham Eagland*)

it could well be the cries of a man wanting the woman he loved by him as he died. It is indeed odd that no accusation was made at the time and the son appears to have treated Jennet with kindness at first.

It was only when he began to suffer loss of goods and cattle that talk of Jennet being a witch arose, and it seems quite feasible that young Lister was seeking a scapegoat for his own mismanagement of his inheritance. In 1612, Jennet was committed to the Lent Assizes at York, accused by Thomas Lister of causing the death by witchcraft of 'a child of one Dodgsonnes'. Oddly, the Dodgsons do not appear to have accused her, and Thomas Lister does not at this time accuse her of causing harm to himself or of being implicated in the death of his father. Jennet was acquitted of the charge for lack of evidence. It is at this point that the Pendle witches come into the picture in the story of Jennet Preston. On the Good Friday immediately after her acquittal Jennet rode to Malkin Tower, the home of Elizabeth Southerns – known as Old Demdike – her widowed daughter Elizabeth Device and her grandchildren Alizon, James and nine-year-old Jennet Device. The Devices made a bare living by begging, casual work and occasional theft. Old Demdike, aged eighty, was recognised as a village healer of people and animals. She used magic with potions and clay images, for ill deeds as well as good. She initiated the whole family into her skills so that they were all familiar with traditional village witchcraft. In addition they were all fond of cats and dogs and were affectionate

Westby Hall Farm, the site of the Lister family home. (*Graham Eagland*)

towards them, which was regarded as odd and suspicious in those days when witches were believed to have familiars in animal form who were their contact with the Devil. They were a family ripe for accusations.

On 18 March, some days before Jennet's visit to Malkin Tower, the teenage Alizon Device met a travelling pedlar, John Law, and begged for some pins. When he refused it would appear that Alizon forcefully expressed her displeasure at this. As she did so, he fell down with a stroke, whereupon he accused her of causing him to become lame by use of witchcraft. She seems to have accepted the blame and begged for his forgiveness, which he apparently gave. However, his son insisted on accusing Alizon and, on 30 March, she was taken to the home of the magistrate Roger Nowell for investigation. Nowell was interested in witchcraft and well-read on the subject but he had many preconceptions about witches, which could well have prejudiced his interpretation of statements that were made to him by the members of the Device family and others who were present at the meeting at Malkin Tower. In the course of these interrogations both James and little Jennet identified Jennet Preston as being there, and James testified that she had asked for aid in causing the death of Thomas Lister. It may be that she was angry with him because of his accusation at the Lent Assizes and that she merely and understandably expressed a wish to see him dead.

Jennet had ridden to that meeting on a white foal and James also apparently stated that when she left she flew on it. Nowell took this animal to be her familiar and that she was able to fly, a skill he believed from his reading that all witches possessed. However, whatever James said was certainly open to alternative interpretations. Whatever the truth of the matter, when Jennet was committed to the Summer Assizes in York, these statements were used against her, and Lister accused her not only of seeking to kill him by her witchcraft but also of having already killed his father by the same means four years before. He claimed that she had touched the corpse and it had bled, which was a sure sign of a witch. As already mentioned, he also interpreted his father's dying words as proof of his belief that he had been bewitched by Jennet Preston. This time Jennet was found guilty and executed in York in July of that year.

Meanwhile Old Demdike – who was to die in prison before coming to trial – Elizabeth and Alizon Device, Anne Whittle, another eighty-year-old (known as Chattox) and her daughter Anne Redferne were incarcerated in Lancaster Castle awaiting trial. For the first time in England, witches were alleged to have met in a coven, something more usually associated with beliefs on the Continent, and charged with having plotted to kill the warder and release Alizon by witchcraft. Like Jennet Preston they too were found guilty and executed in August 1612.

But there was simply no evidence or suggestion that Jennet Preston had ever done as the others had undoubtedly done, no proof that she had practised as a wise woman, cast spells, made potions or images or cursed anyone. Her sole accuser was Thomas Lister. She went to her death without confession or penitence. Her husband and her supporters in Gisburn were unafraid to voice their indignation at the obsession and prejudice of the magistrates and judiciary, which had made her the victim, for whatever reason, of one man's animosity toward her.

The 'snow witch' on Pendle Hill near Gisburn.

Elizabeth Roberts, 1654

The belief that witches could change themselves into animal form was not as strong and widespread in Yorkshire as it was in other parts of the country, such as East Anglia. Where it did exist, the animal most usually favoured was the hare, as seen in stories of the hare-witches of the North York Moors. The question of witches having 'familiars' was a different matter; the most popular animals in that case were the cat or dog. The following story involves a cat but not as a 'familiar'.

In October 1654, John Greenliffe, a cordwainer from Beverley in the East Riding, accused Elizabeth Roberts, the wife of a joiner, also of Beverley, of tormenting him with witchcraft. He claimed that she did so after first appearing to him in her usual clothes and wearing a ruff, but he had then seen her take on the form of a cat. She clawed so firmly onto his leg, he said, that for quite some time he was unable to release it. She attacked him while lying on top of him in his bed and struck him on the head, causing him to fall into a trance. When he recovered his senses he saw her leaving his room once more in her human form and wearing her usual apparel. She then escaped over a wall. As a result of these attacks he was much plagued with pains in his head.

He went on to testify that on yet another occasion she appeared and tormented him in the shape of a bee, and threw him around from place to place so violently that five or six men were unable to hold him. This is a most unusual creature to find associated with a witch, but one that could well cause a body to twist and turn from place to place. I am sure that we have all seen a nervous person fling themselves around in an endeavour to escape the attentions of a determined bee or wasp.

What could have caused John Greenliffe to make such accusations? Could it possibly have been that he really did believe himself to be bewitched? Was he perhaps suffering from a delusional illness or did he have some grudge against Elizabeth? Or had he perhaps been in an illicit relationship with her and was using this charge to deny it and cover it up? We shall never know. We can only speculate.

There seems to be no record of a verdict or a sentence following these strange accusations and so perhaps we can assume that Elizabeth Roberts was acquitted.

The old gateway to Beverley. (*Graham Eagland*)

Mother Shipton, 1488–1561

The picturesque town of Knaresborough in North Yorkshire is a popular place for visitors. A pleasant wooded pathway, the Long Walk, running alongside the River Nidd on the opposite side from the castle, takes them to their destination. They come to see the strange Dropping Well festooned with objects such as hats, gloves, shoes, teddy bears and other toys, all turned to stone by the elements in the water which runs down the rock face and drops on to them as they hang below. It is also sometimes known as Mother Shipton's Well, for close by is a small, damp cave where one stormy summer's night in 1488 Ursula Sonteil, the baby girl who was to grow up to become one of England's most famous witches, is reputed to have been born. She was sadly deformed with a crooked spine and possibly a humpback. It is said that at a later date her unprepossessing appearance helped to form the stereotype of a witch as an ugly old woman. In 1599, the Archbishop of York, Simon Harsnett, described a witch as being an old crone leaning on a staff, bent, toothless, hollow-eyed, trembling and muttering in the streets, with a sharp tongue; a description which could surely be applied to many an old woman.

Ursula's mother, Agatha, was an orphan aged only fifteen when the baby was born. As she has been described as idle, with no mention of any occupation, it is possible that she was a prostitute. Certainly when she was pregnant she was taken before the local Justice of the Peace on a charge of prostitution. Agatha seems to have been a girl of some mettle. She was in no way bowed down by the accusation or awed by her judge, and pointed out that not one but two of his own servants were at that very moment pregnant and he was the father. The court was shocked and the case dismissed. It was rumoured that Agatha had been seduced by a handsome charmer or wise man who continued to support her in some comfort as his lover. Also, the Abbot of Beverley surprisingly baptised Ursula despite her illegitimacy, and continued to have contact with her through the years. However, the circumstances of her birth remain a mystery and little is known of

The cave where Mother Shipton was born. (*Graham Eagland*)

her childhood, although from an early age she was called a witch and a child of the Devil. Agatha gave Ursula at the age of two into the care of a foster mother and spent the rest of her life in a convent in Nottingham. Ursula played many mischievous tricks on her foster mother and gossip grew of her contact with the Devil.

As she grew up she learned the use of herbs and potions, and used that knowledge to help people. She cured their ailments and those of their animals, and healed their wounds by what they may have seen as her witch's magic and spells. The wooded area beside the Long Walk may well have provided some of the medicinal plants and roots that she needed, and the water from the Dropping Well, with its special properties, possibly played a part in some of her potions. Although she is always known as a witch, she might better be described as a wise woman. At the age of twenty-four, despite an appearance that some would have considered a severe impediment to wedlock, she married Toby Shipton, a carpenter. Some thought she made use of a love potion to bewitch her husband, while another rumour said that she had money that provided the attraction. Whatever the truth of the matter, she and her husband appear to have lived contentedly together and, although she was never to have children, Ursula Sonteil became known as Mother Shipton.

Her fame grew and spread, not just locally or throughout the North, but nationwide, and her name is remembered today chiefly for her predictions. But how many of those predictions are truly attributable to Mother Shipton herself?

The figure of Mother Shipton carved within her cave. (*Graham Eagland*)

Like the prophecies of Nostradamus they are couched in such terms that they can be interpreted to fit many different events and their outcome. There are no written accounts of them before 1641, but since then no less than fifty books have been written about her and her prophecies, with new ones often being added.

One of the earliest written reports of her sayings and predictions claims that they were told by Mother Shipton herself, shortly before her death, to a young girl by the name of Joanne Waller. When a woman told Mother Shipton that a smock and a petticoat had been stolen, a severe loss in those days, she was told not to worry. Mother Shipton said that she knew who had taken them and that the thief would confess and return them, which indeed she did on the next market day. But can we be sure that Mother Shipton didn't merely have a strong idea who might be the thief, and had frightened her with her magic powers if she didn't do just that? Again, when a young nobleman, anxious for his inheritance, came to ask her if she would tell him when his father would die, she sent him away unanswered. The young man then fell ill and his father came to ask Mother Shipton if his son would recover. Her reply to him was, 'Those who gape out for others' death, their own unlooked for comes about'. She may simply have known that what ailed him was fatal but, when the young man died, her reputation for possessing the power to foretell grew, causing both fear and respect.

Among the many things she is said to have foretold was piped water to the citizens of York, with the words, 'Water shall come over Ouze Bridge, and a windmill shall be set upon a tower, and an Elm Tree shall lie at every man's door.' York did eventually get its piped water from the Ouse near Lendal Bridge, in pipes of hollowed-out tree trunks, which are still preserved in the Castle Museum in York to this day. Mother Shipton was an intelligent woman who could perhaps just see that to do such a thing was a possibility. On national matters she is said to have discussed and foretold the Dissolution of the Monasteries with the Abbot of Beverley, and King Henry's success against the French. She made an enemy of Cardinal Wolsey whom she called the Mitred Peacock, and he sent men to threaten her and silence her but she was unafraid. Wolsey was journeying from London to York and swore she would burn when he arrived in York. Mother Shipton said that he might see York but he would never reach it. He arrived at his palace at Cawood, south of York, but was arrested there for treason and taken back to London. He was already ill and died at Leicester on the way.

Perhaps the most famously quoted of her supposed predictions is the one that includes the words, 'the world to an end shall come in eighteen hundred and eighty-one'. It is one of a hundred rhyming couplets capable of interpretation as predictions of all manner of modern events. 'Carriages without horses shall go' can be taken to refer to the invention of the motor car. 'Under water men shall walk, shall ride, shall sleep, shall talk,' must surely predict the submarine, and 'Iron in the water shall float, as easy as a wooden boat,' must indicate the coming of the steam boat and the modern great liners. These and others like them appeared in a work of 1862 that purported to be a reprint of a very early book, but it was written in a language that quite clearly does not belong to the sixteenth century. It was finally exposed as the invention of one Charles Hindley who admitted to the deception. It is ironic that the most popular and best-known predictions should be the very ones that we know without doubt are ones that were not made by Mother Shipton.

But despite our lack of proof, or certain knowledge of the life and true predictions of Mother Shipton, she became one of England's most famous witches during the seventeenth-century witch craze, and has remained so over the years. Many pubs were given her name in the past but there are only two remaining. One of them, appropriately enough, is in her home town of Knaresborough. Unusually, a moth found in Yorkshire also bears her name, the pattern on its wings said to resemble her profile. It seems that the name of Mother Shipton will never be forgotten.

Mary Sykes, 1650

What was it about widows that caused them so often to be regarded and accused as witches? Whatever the reason, it is a fact that those accused of witchcraft were very often poor widows. Without a husband to support and protect them they would be reduced to using any means of survival that they could. Perhaps it served their purpose to claim to have special powers. Some turned to begging and no doubt were given food or money in fear of what a refusal might bring. And yet this probably aroused resentment in the giver. With such poverty, their living conditions, appearance and even their mental state could deteriorate. They were simply people who were outside the normal conformity of life. In an age when early death was commonplace, those who were accused need not necessarily have fitted the stereotype of a gnarled old crone as described by Simon Harsnett, Archbishop of York in 1599. But times were hard for many and especially for a poor widow. We may assume that people aged more quickly than we do today.

We do not know the age or the appearance of Mary Sykes of Bowling near Bradford, but we do know that she was a widow when she was accused of witchcraft in 1650. Her accuser, Dorothy Rhodes, was also a widow but seems to have been of somewhat higher social status. This again tends often to be the pattern in cases of witchcraft – the accuser comes from a slightly superior social class to the accused. Mrs Rhodes made her accusation before Mr Henry Tempest, a Justice of the Peace, on 18 March. She told how a week before on the Sunday, she and her daughter Sarah, and a young child were in bed together. They had all been asleep for a while when Mrs Rhodes was woken by Sarah who was obviously distressed, 'quakeing and holding her hands together'. When asked what was troubling her, she replied that 'Mary Sykes came in att a hole att the bedd feete' onto the bed, took her by the throat and tried to thrust her fingers into her mouth to choke her. When asked by her mother why she had not cried out, she replied that she could not speak because she was being choked. She added that Mary Sykes had touched her in the street and rendered her speechless. What could perhaps have been seen as a bad dream caused by fright at an encounter with a reputed witch, was seen as indication of bewitchment.

Sarah complained of visits not only from Mary Sykes. She also claimed that a Mrs Kellett came with the other woman. When she was reminded that Mrs Kellett had been dead for two years Sarah said, 'Ah Mother, but she never rests for she appeared to me the foulest fiend that ever I saw with a pair of eyes like saucers.' She had given her, she said, 'a box of the ear' through the opening in the wall, which 'made the fire flash out of my eyes'. Mrs Rhodes went on to describe how Sarah had, several times since that Sunday, suffered from pains and numbness, sometimes as often as six times a day. Her joints seized up so that she could not move and also she could not speak. These fits lasted sometimes as long as an hour and, when Sarah recovered, she always insisted that it was Mary Sykes who had caused them.

Richard Booth of Bolling testified that he had seen Sarah Rhodes several times when she was being troubled in this way, 'quaking and dithering' and unable to speak. Mary Sykes, he said, had also many times told him that she would 'cross' him, and he had lost a great deal due to deaths among his cattle. Henry Cordingley of Tong also gave evidence that Mary Sykes had threatened to make his beasts fewer. One midnight, when he went to fodder his horses, he found Mary Sykes riding on one of his cows, which were near the horses. He tried to strike her but stumbled and fell and she escaped through a window. He actually stated that he saw her fly through the window. Since many believed that all witches could fly, it may be that, when Mary Sykes (always assuming that she was actually there) rushed towards the window and leapt through it, Henry Cordingly saw what he expected to see. He was sincere in his statement that he had seen her fly. He went on to describe how one of his horses, a valuable one worth the then considerable sum of £4 16s, became ill. After 'dithering and quaking', it died within a few days and on being opened was found to have so little blood that it would not have filled an eggshell. Cordingley became convinced that Mary Sykes had bewitched his animals. Another animal had suffered in the same way, but had recovered after Mary was examined.

William Rhodes of Bowling testified that he had been in Mary Sykes' house and heard her say that 'Henry Cordingley brags of his daughters, what gay daughters they are'. According to Rhodes, she then went on to say that she had already had his eldest daughter 'off her feet at once', but swore that 'she shall be taken off her feet and made a miracle'. This would appear to be a threat of causing illness and possibly death.

Women were appointed by the authorities to examine Mary's body for the witch-mark. They found on her buttock a red lump about the 'bignesse of a nut', which oozed moisture like lye when squeezed. Also on her left side, close to her arm a wart-like lump that could be pulled out to a length of half an inch was found. Such blemishes were usually taken to be certain proof that a woman was a witch. Yet on this occasion, despite the fact that she had two such strange and unfamiliar marks on her body, and the testimonies against her, Mary Sykes was lucky. She was arraigned but acquitted.

The Timble Witches, 1621

The tiny village of Timble in the Harrogate district of North Yorkshire, situated in the Washburn valley and close to both the Swinsty and Fewston reservoirs, lends its name to the six women accused by Edward Fairfax of Fewston of bewitching his daughters. Edward Fairfax came from an illustrious family. He was the third son of Sir Thomas Fairfax, knighted by Queen Elizabeth in 1576. Both of his brothers were soldiers: Charles was killed in action in 1604 and Thomas also distinguished himself in the wars on the Continent, was knighted at Rouen, and later became involved in diplomatic affairs. When his father died in 1599 he inherited his estates at Denton and the military tradition continued in the family through the generations. His son Fernando and his grandson Thomas Fairfax fought in the Civil War. Indeed, Black Tom, as he was known, became Commander-in-Chief of Cromwell's army, although he was later involved in the restoration of Charles II. Both Edward's sisters married well. Ursula became the wife of Sir Henry Bellasis. In the north aisle of York Minster, a fine memorial shows her kneeling in prayer beside her husband. Christiana married John Aske of Aughton, a descendant of Robert Aske, who led the Pilgrimage of Grace – the rising in the North against Henry VIII's Dissolution of the Monasteries – and was executed in 1537. During the Civil War, the Bellasis and the Fairfax families found themselves on opposing sides.

Edward Fairfax was quite unlike his brothers. He was of a shy and retiring nature with no inclination towards the military life or that of the court. He was a scholar who preferred the quiet life, and if he sought renown at all it was through his writings and poetry. He was one of the founders of the Modern School of English Poetry, in the company of such great poets as Edmund Spenser, and translated and published the Italian Torquato Tasso's poem 'Jerusalem Delivered' in 1600. Very little is known of his life before this time. It seems likely that he was born at Denton and may well have been educated in Leeds. Wherever that may have been he was well educated and he became a fine scholar. He married a Miss Laycock

The tiny village of Timble today. (*Graham Eagland*)

from the village of Copmanthorpe on the outskirts of York and moved around 1600 to Newhall in the Washburn valley – a house later to be lost under the waters of the Swinsty reservoir. His daughter, Elizabeth, was presumably born here as she is recorded as being baptised at Fewston in 1606. In 1607 he appears to have been living in Leeds but, in 1619, he returned with his family to Newhall. He remained there until his death in 1635.

It was during the two years following the family's return to Newhall that the Fairfax girls began to experience 'strange disorders' of fits and trance-like states, which their father described and published in his extraordinary book entitled *Daemonalogia; a discourse on witchcraft as it was acted out in the Family of Mr Edward Fairfax of Fuystone in the County of York in the year 1621*, in which he described in great detail his supposed evidence of spells and black magic and related how his daughters had been bewitched. Helen Fairfax in one of her early fits described seeing a well-dressed gentleman who proposed marriage to her and promised that he would make her queen but reacted with fear at the mention of God. At another time she imagined she was speaking to one of the witches tormenting her and asked her how she became a witch. The witch in her imagination told her that she had made a pact with a man she had met upon the moor. Helen, who was twenty-one at the time of these strange fits, was described as being 'slow of speech' and had difficulty in learning things. With the benefit of hindsight and modern knowledge it seems extremely likely that the cause of these occurrences as he describes them was epilepsy. The kind known as *petit mal* produces brief trance-like episodes when the person appears to be daydreaming with a blank expression and is unaware of doing so. This is the form that most commonly affects children. *Grand mal*, with fits and foaming at the mouth, is more dramatic and, although it is more generally an adult affliction, it can also occasionally occur alongside *petit mal*. If this was indeed the sickness from which his daughters were suffering, it is perhaps not surprising, in a period when witchcraft was believed in and thought to be rife, that a suspicious and prickly man who did not understand his neighbours, such as Fairfax, should conclude that they were bewitched; although perhaps a scholar of his character could have been expected to think otherwise. When his youngest daughter Ann died, Fairfax openly accused six women of the neighbourhood of a conspiracy of witchcraft against his family, and despite the advice of Henry Graves, the Vicar of Fewston, he had them arrested and taken for trial to York. Before the accusations, it is worth noting that his daughters Elizabeth and Helen and baby Ann seem to have spent time happily and unafraid in the care and company of these women. Oddly, despite his obvious dislike and snobbish disdain for his neighbours, describing them as 'rude people' who used 'wise men and wizards to treat their animals' ailments', Fairfax himself seems to have made no attempt to bar them from his daughters' presence.

The site of Fairfax's house now lies beneath the waters of Swinsty Reservoir. (*Graham Eagland*)

Jennet Dibble, an aged widow, was considered by him to be the ringleader of the group and was a member of a family with a long-lasting reputation as witches. This may well have been true because, as we have seen throughout this book, many villages had their local witch or so-called 'wise woman' who practised rural witchcraft with herbs, potions and spells. She treated ailments of both people and animals, told fortunes and supposedly used her powers to solve people's problems. In this case, Fairfax declared that a large black cat called Gibbe was her 'familiar', the connection to the Devil that witches were believed to have, and which he claimed 'hath attended her now above forty years'. This seems a particularly ridiculous claim. Jennet may well have had a cat for that number of years but it would be a truly supernatural cat were the same one to live so long.

Marjery Thorpe, also a widow, was said to have a familiar in the shape of a yellow bird named Tewhit, the name given to the lapwing in Yorkshire. She was accused of having made and thrown images of the children into water. The making of such images was said to be a common practice of witches, and they were then used in various ways to bring about harm to the person depicted. These images, which were called 'pictures' by the women, were possibly actually wax or clay 'dolls' used in black magic to bewitch the girls. Fairfax certainly believed so. Described also by the girls as 'pictures', the figures were naked apart from the Fairfax girls'. Helen was depicted in her usual dress with a white hat and her hair hanging down in curls around her ears. Her sisters were also clothed in their usual attire. Marjery Thorpe had carved their names into bread as a means of obtaining mysterious signs, according to Fairfax's allegation. Yet another widow was Margaret Waite who, it was said, had come to live in the area with a reputation as a witch. Fairfax also denounced her as a thief as she had had a pennyworth of grain from him for which she had failed to pay. Her daughter was declared impudent and of lewd behaviour and accused by Fairfax along with her mother.

Elizabeth Fletcher, or Foster, he denounced as having great power over one of his wealthy neighbours, as well as blaming her for his daughter Elizabeth's fall from a hay mow simply because she was watching her at the time. The reference to the wealthy neighbour was to the Robinsons at Swinsty Hall. Henry Robinson was a moneylender who had acquired Swinsty Hall in 1590 as the result of a foreclosure on a mortgage. His wife appears to have had suicidal or even homicidal episodes for which he would call on the aid and skills of Elizabeth Fletcher. The last of those accused by Fairfax was a woman by the name of Elizabeth Dickenson, who, he said, had also bewitched the daughter of another neighbour, Maud Jeffray. When the women showed the images that they were said to use in their bewitchings to the girls Helen had remarked that theirs had rosy cheeks but one was very pale. According to Fairfax, she was told that that was Maud Jeffray. However, close questioning of Maud established that she had been coached by her father to simulate fits of a similar nature to those of the Fairfax girls, and he was sent to prison as a result. In addition to his general accusation of bewitchment, Fairfax claimed that the three girls had been abducted by the women and forced to take part in a pagan ceremony, a Beltane Feast, on the moor at midnight on Midsummer's Eve.

It was some time after this that his youngest daughter died, of what we do not know, and it was this that was the catalyst for Fairfax's allegations. The women were twice brought before the court but each time they were acquitted for lack of concrete evidence. The Reverend Graves vouched for their good characters. On their release and return home, a great celebration was arranged, with a huge feast on Timble Gill in which the whole village seems to have been involved. This took place on 10 April 1621, the Thursday before Good Friday, and continued through the night until dawn. It must have been a great relief to the women to be cleared of the charge of indulging in such malign practices, especially at a time when witches were suspected and condemned everywhere, often on flimsy evidence. A joyful celebration with friends and family and neighbours seems a not unreasonable reaction. However, in Fairfax's jaundiced and superstitious view, it was a witches' feast with the Devil himself at the head of the table. There is no possibility that the six women could have been responsible for any of the things alleged by Fairfax. However, deep in the wild countryside, the people of Timble may well have been lacking in their knowledge and practice of the Christian religion as Fairfax saw it. They may have clung to old ways and beliefs of village lore and pagan festivals that were beyond his understanding and acceptance as a refined and educated man of puritan persuasion. The Revd Graves for his part appears to have come to an understanding and appreciation of his parishioners of which Fairfax proved quite incapable.

It seems strange that as he so disliked his rustic neighbours, and was unable to get on with them, he did not move away from the area. We have no knowledge of relations between them over the following years but we do know that he was still at Newhall when he died fourteen years later.

William and Mary Wade

It was very often the case in accusations of witchcraft and bewitchment that the accuser was a person of higher status in the community than the accused. This was very much so when Elizabeth Mallory accused husband and wife William and Mary Wade in 1654 of having bewitched her. The Wades were not poor people but Elizabeth was the fourteen-year-old daughter of Sir John Mallory, MP for Ripon. The Mallory family had owned the Studley Royal Estate from the middle of the fifteenth century until 1667 when it became the property of the Ainslie family through the marriage of George Ainslie to Mary Mallory, the younger daughter of Sir John who died without a male heir. Sir John had been a Royalist during the Civil War when he held Skipton Castle against Cromwell for three years, but he seems to have adapted to life in the Commonwealth without undue loss of wealth or status.

Another factor often involved in accusations was a prior argument or disagreement, a 'falling-out' between the protagonists. In this case, however, Elizabeth Mallory scarcely knew Mr and Mrs Wade, though they lived near her home of Studley Hall and may well have been tenants of the Mallorys (Studley Hall was destroyed by fire in 1716 and its replacement was also burned down in 1946). Elizabeth had met Mary Wade once when accompanying her mother to the Wades' cottage. Mrs Wade on this occasion offered her visitors some nuts by way of polite refreshment. Elizabeth's only other contact appears to have been an encounter in the dairy at the hall, when Mary Wade jokingly begged for some of the hall-baked bread, saying that she had heard such stories of its high quality and would like to taste it for herself. These seemingly trivial details were given some significance when Mary came before the court, as the belief was that giving food to a witch or receiving food from her gave her power over you.

Not long after this meeting Elizabeth became ill with trembling fits and lost the use of her legs. Oddly she seems to have been able to foretell the onset of these attacks, informing people that she was about to be ill. This went on for several months. She declared with certainty that she was bewitched, but at first did not accuse anyone. When asked who might be tormenting her she replied that 'she knewe not but only trusted in God and desired them to pray with her'.

Later, during one of these fits, Elizabeth suddenly screamed, 'She comes! Mary comes!' The servant who was tending her naturally asked who it was who seemed to be troubling her, but Elizabeth only continued saying, 'Mary comes' over and over again. The servant then began to go through all those that they knew with the name of Mary. When she came to the name Mary Wade, Elizabeth wept and screamed in apparent terror, and so, of course, it seemed obvious that Mary Wade was a witch and responsible for Elizabeth's woes. She told her mother when her fit had subsided that she was sure Mary Wade had bewitched her, but that if Mary would come and admit it and ask for forgiveness, she knew she would be well again.

Lady Mallory sent for Mary and asked her to do what Elizabeth wanted. Not surprisingly she was reluctant to do so. She could hardly be expected to declare herself to be a witch. However, Lady Mallory finally persuaded her by saying that it was simply to help Elizabeth. She did what she was asked and Elizabeth immediately declared that she was cured. Unfortunately, she later found out that Mary had actually only gone through the motions, and had assured Lady Mallory and others that she was no witch and had never cast a spell to bewitch anyone. Elizabeth then declared, 'If she denies it I shall be ill again' and immediately the trembling fits recurred. She also began to vomit many strange objects such as blotting paper, feathers, pins and a stick. Such vomiting was believed to be the sign of an illness induced by a witch. At this point Elizabeth involved Mary's husband William by crying out, 'William, thou terrifier' when in one of her fits. Lady Mallory duly sent for William and made the same request that she had made to his wife. William, however, steadfastly refused to confess, saying he had nothing to confess. Though he was prepared to agree that Elizabeth was possessed of an evil spirit, he denied any responsibility for her illness.

Sir John and Lady Mallory were nevertheless convinced that Elizabeth was bewitched by William and Mary Wade. Husband and wife were arrested, jailed and brought before the court at York. When Elizabeth knew that they were imprisoned, she recovered. The details of the case are on record but we do not know what verdict was reached. It is possible that the judges were sceptical about the whole affair and they were acquitted. It was not unknown for children to pretend illness. In 1622, in York, John Jeffray was sent to prison for fraud after accusing a group of women against whom he had a grudge of bewitching his daughter. On examination it turned out that the child had been coached by her father to simulate illness. Although the parents were almost certainly innocent in this case, it seems highly likely that Elizabeth Mallory's illness was not real. Why she acted as she did is not clear. Perhaps she had a grudge against the Wades which is unknown to us. Or was her behaviour just that of a spoilt and manipulative child? Was it aimed, for some reason, at her mother and came to involve the Wades simply because of the chance mention of their name by the servant?

Hannah Waugh

When a murder was committed at Anngrove Hall in 1830, Hannah Waugh, the Broughton witch, used her powers to expose and punish the murderer who would never otherwise have paid for his crime. In doing so she earned herself a place in local legend. The Hall (also known as the Old Manor House) lay on the road between Stokesley and Ayton. The Squire there had a beautiful daughter who had fallen in love with his under-coachman, Henry Edwards. They were secretly engaged. The Squire found out but would not countenance such an unsuitable match and forbade them to see each other. His words were to no avail. The Squire then sent Henry on an errand to Stokesley to deliver a box of silver and jewellery to a gentleman about to catch the coach to London. After an appropriate time he enquired whether Henry had returned but was told that he had not. It eventually became clear that the coachman was not going to appear. The Squire claimed that it was plain that he had stolen the valuables and made off. He called for his horse and rode off, not to Stokesley but to Thirsk some distance away. He spent the day making enquiries and offered a reward of £200 for any information. But no information about either the man or the jewellery was forthcoming. Everyone was very shocked and surprised that Henry Edwards who had seemed such an honest and decent young man should have done such a thing.

As the months went by, interest in the affair faded. Only one person could not forget: Henry's sister Polly, who worked as a servant at the Grange, a big house at Great Ayton, never believed that the brother that she loved and knew so well would ever stoop to theft. She felt sure that something dreadful had happened to him and was convinced one day that she saw his ghost with his head battered in. This is where Hannah Waugh comes into the picture. Polly was so frightened and worried that she went to her for help and advice in finding her brother's murderer.

Hannah advised Polly to obtain a horseshoe from a horse which her brother had ridden. It was to be placed in a prominent position where many people could see it, and should the murderer happen to glance at it he would immediately become ill. Thus he would betray his guilt. Polly managed to persuade the coachman at Anngrove to give her a shoe from Henry's favourite horse with the intention of putting it on the wall of the inn at Stokesley. She thought that would be a good place to catch the eye of a large number of people. She had no chance to get away immediately to do so and, in the meantime, she put it on a wall at the Grange where she worked.

Quite by chance her employer was entertaining guests to a card party that evening and among those invited was the Squire of Anngrove. As he arrived he glanced at the horseshoe and turned pale and began to tremble and became suddenly ill. As he was driven home Polly shouted at him, 'Who murdered Henry Edwards?' It was obvious to her that the whole business of the stolen jewellery was a charade to cover up the Squire's crime in getting rid of his daughter's unwelcome suitor. However, the Squire was an influential man and Polly was warned to hold her tongue.

This she did but Hannah Waugh had no fear of him and took a hand. When next she met him in Stokesley market place she cursed him with the following words:

You've had your day
But lambs will play
And skip where Anngrove stands
No lime shall hod
Its stones, no sod
Shall wrap up the deed of thy hands.

Gradually the word got around and suspicions grew. The locals took against him and his servants left one by one till none were left. The Squire could find no replacements willing to go to work at the Hall. With no one to work the land or look after the house, it fell into wrack and ruin until finally Hannah's words came true. A broken man, the Squire left, and some time afterwards the remains of the unfortunate coachman were found buried in the grounds of the ruined Hall.

Anne Wilkinson, 1670

In the seventeenth century there were plenty of people who, although they might believe in witchcraft, or at the least have ambivalent feelings about it, nonetheless sought their protection from it in religion rather than the Law. They put their trust in the power of God and of prayer, believing it to be stronger than the power of witches or of the Devil. When Margaret Wilson returned home in tears and full of fear after she had been cursed by Anne Wilkinson, her mother 'bad her put her trust in God', and to hope that she would then come to no harm. This advice seems to have been of no comfort to Margaret.

Anne Wilkinson lived in the small village of Alne, a few miles from the market town of Easingwold in the North Riding. As was so often the case with those believed to be witches, she was a widow. When Mary Earneley, the daughter of John Earneley of Alne, fell ill she cried out that Anne Wilkinson was pricking her with pins and kept slapping her thighs, as though that was the area in which she felt the pricking. At other times her cry of complaint was that Anne had 'run a spitt into her'. Mary's father then sent for Anne Wilkinson, to confront her. When Anne arrived, Mary became very agitated and shouted, 'Burne her! Burne her! Shee tormented two of my sisters.' This information was given in a deposition by one Ann Mattson before Frank Driffield Esq. on 1 April 1670 in York. She added that two of Mary's sisters had died 'since Candlemasse last', and, just before one of them died, a black ribbon with a crooked pin in it was found and removed from her mouth. Who this Anne Mattson was, we do not learn. Whether she was a relative, or perhaps someone who was taking care of and nursing Mary, is not stated. Nor do we know what age Mary was. Oddly, neither parent seems to have given evidence. Could it be that they did not really believe that witchcraft was involved? Perhaps when the father sent for Anne Wilkinson, he did so in order, with her help, to convince Mary that she was mistaken?

George Wrightson, also of Alne, confirmed what had been stated by Ann Mattson. He added that, when Mary was writhing and crying with pain, Mrs

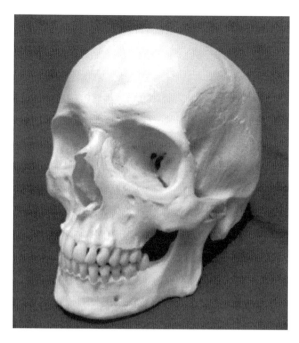

A skull was a useful ingredient in casting spells.

Earneley sent him, together with other neighbours, to Anne Wilkinson's cottage, hoping to catch her in the act of casting a spell. He had to report, however, that he found Anne sitting quietly by her fire, doing nothing that could be construed as casting a magic spell. Nor was there anything visible that could be used for such a purpose. Was this perhaps what Mrs Earneley had expected, and her purpose in sending them was to convince both Mary and the neighbours that Anne was not involved? It seems plausible and adds to the possibility that Mary's parents were not convinced that witchcraft was involved in their daughter's illness.

Anne, when called to defend herself, declared that she had never done anything to harm Mr Earneley or any of his family, and would never do so. As to the bewitching of any of his children, she said that she was 'sacklesse' – an old word meaning 'innocent of ill intent'. (Now understood to mean 'ineffectual' or 'simple-minded' in the Yorkshire dialect.) Although she had done nothing about it at the time, Margaret Wilson then came forward to tell of an occasion some years before when her meeting with Anne Wilkinson led to an altercation that ended with Anne cursing her and wishing 'she might never thrive'. Margaret had lost some money from her purse, and was accused by Anne of going to a wise man for help in finding it – a skill which was part of the repertoire of most wise men. She had got him to raise a great wind, Anne said, which had affected her eyes. It is not clear what exactly the supposed purpose of this great wind was, or why Anne should be angry that Margaret had been to a wise man and had got her money back. Had she been responsible for its loss or been accused of being so? Maybe she felt that Margaret should have gone to her for help. Whatever the reason, according to Margaret it put her into a great rage. The next day after this incident, when Margaret churned the butter it wouldn't turn and she blamed this on Anne's evil influence. She said that she then fell sick – though in what way she does not specify – and was ill for two years until a Scottish physician came to the next village of Tollerton. He told her that she was bewitched and presumably cured her though she does not say so. She went on to add that her then husband, John Akers, who had previously been strong and healthy, became ill with a lingering disease, and eventually died.

In spite of all this testimony, Anne Wilkinson was acquitted. It seems that she made a favourable impression on the court. There was no real evidence of any wrongdoing and she was believed when she declared herself 'sacklesse'. There is no record of whether this was believed by the villagers, or of what Anne's reception was like back in the village. We are also left in the dark regarding the outcome of Mary Earneley's illness. Did she succumb to the same illness that had carried of her two sisters? Or did she recover from what may simply have been some temporary and normal ailment, and an obsession that she had been bewitched?

A Miscellany of Other Witches

The previous pages of this book tell of women and men whose stories can be found in official records: depositions and other accounts of the times; stories of witchcraft, magic and spells, of reputations, accusations and even execution. There are many others about whom very little is known beyond a simple statement of a name, a date and an accusation. In many cases we are left to speculate and fill in the details for ourselves.

Unnamed Witch, 1279

In 1279 John de Kerneslawe killed an unnamed witch who entered his house. For what purpose she was there we do not know, nor do we know whether the killing was deliberate or accidental. We do know that her body was burned by the local clergy, but no mention is made of any punishment for John de Kerneslawe. The killing was presumably deemed to be justified. In these early times witchcraft was regarded as heresy and the work of the Devil, to be dealt with by the Church rather than the Law.

Godfrey Darel, 1286

Godfrey Darel, a monk in the Cistercian Abbey at Rievaulx, was reported to the Archbishop of York in 1286 and accused of witchcraft. There is no information as to what form his witchcraft took. The monasteries were places where there were often learned and skilled men. Perhaps he was guilty of dabbling in experiments in medicines and potions which were seen by others as spells or magic. Perhaps his religious observances were unorthodox. He may even have prayed to the Devil, or indulged in what were considered 'unnatural practices'. Frustratingly, his exact offence is hidden from us, as is the Archbishop's verdict. It is interesting to realise that accusations of witchcraft were to be found even in a house of religion.

Lady Jane Cholmley, 1570

Sir Francis Cholmley and his wife came to live in Whitby in 1570 when he inherited his father's estate. His wife Jane was very unpopular and Sir Francis's family disapproved of her strongly. This may well have been because of her reputation as a witch. On the other hand that reputation may have grown out of their dislike of her. A later member of the family, Sir Hugh Cholmley, in memoirs written in the 1650s, was of the opinion that 'Francis Cholmley was exceedingly overtopped and guided by his wife which it is thought she did by witchcraft or some extraordinary means'. Sir Francis died in 1579 and Lady Jane was rumoured to have somehow been involved in his death. She was fortunate that she was never brought to face charges in court for any of her supposed witching activities, as the sixteenth century was a time when witches were much feared. Her immunity to prosecution may have been due to her title, although even far greater titles were not necessarily guarantees of freedom from accusation. More than a century earlier, Elizabeth Woodville, the queen of Edward IV, and her mother were both accused of being witches.

Cuthbert Williamson, 1594

The parish records of York show that in 1594 a certain Cuthbert Williamson, a local wise man or Cunning-man, was brought before the Church Court on a charge of witchcraft. Williamson was clearly a man who was thought able to detect when people were bewitched, but this skill, in itself, was enough to suggest to the authorities that he was a witch himself. In the course of his examination the question was put to him as to 'how he knoweth when one is forspoken' (i.e. bewitched). His reply is recorded in Tudor Parish Documents of the Diocese of York, edited by Canon J. S. Purvis in 1948. His strange, and one would have thought unreliable, method was, so he said, 'so sone as his help is craved, in that case his eies will forthwith run with water'. This suggests that in fact he simply went along with the person who was seeking help and who believed that he or she was suffering from bewitchment. One cannot help wondering if Williamson, like some actors, was able to shed tears as required, or whether he had some eye problem which he made use of as a part of his diagnostic tools.

Elizabeth Melton, 1597

As we have seen throughout this book, very few witches were executed in Yorkshire, certainly in comparison with other counties such as East Anglia. Even those who were found guilty were often punished by imprisonment or lesser means. Many were found not guilty and acquitted. Elizabeth Melton of Collingham near Wetherby was found guilty in 1597, though there is no record of the exact details of what her offence was as a witch. What is on record is that she was found guilty and condemned. Whether that was to death or to imprisonment is not made clear but the use of the word 'condemned' strongly suggests that the verdict was death.

Whether it was death or incarceration to which the judge sentenced her, Elizabeth was eventually spared her punishment. There is a record that she was granted a pardon by the Privy Council, although no statement as to why she was given mercy. We can only speculate.

A Bewitchment in 1601

A common accusation in the stories of witchcraft was that of causing fits by bewitchment. Such was the case with Marmaduke Jackson of Bishop Burton in the East Riding, 1601. His fits took an incredible form. He was said to have been thrown into the fire by an unseen force, yet he seems to have been unburnt by this. This same mysterious force then caused him to be raised as high as six feet into the air and spun and twisted around, after which he fell and landed heavily on his head. Despite the fact that one would expect serious injury from a fall onto the head from such a height, he escaped any injury or hurt. The only effect following these unusual and vigorous actions was that 'he lyeth in a dead swound half an hour except it be by a bed then in despite of ten men he shall be drawn under ye bed by ye heels'. Since it seems unlikely that there would be ten men around young Marmaduke during his fits, we may assume that this was meant only to convey the impossibility of resistance to the mysterious force that drew him under the bed. Stranger still he was said to 'gallop upon his knees and hands faster yn a man can run'. Throughout his ordeals, Marmaduke knew where the two supposed witches who had bewitched him were and could describe what they were doing. The two women suspected of the bewitchment confessed to their supposed crime, yet unusually this did not lead to any improvement in Marmaduke's condition, as would have been expected. 'The Devil leaveth not from tormenting him', the record states.

The parish records for Bishop Burton show that an Anthony Jackson and his wife Margaret had a son named Marmaduke in 1578. Could this possibly be the Marmaduke Jackson involved in the case in 1601? It would mean that he would have been aged twenty-three at the time, yet reference is made to him as a boy in the case. Perhaps the term was used merely to indicate his youth and may well have been common usage at the time. It does seem an unlikely and extraordinary coincidence if there were two Marmaduke Jacksons in Bishop Burton within that space of time.

Jane Blomely, 1623

Frances Craven, the wife of Marmaduke Craven, a yeoman farmer of Doncaster, became ill on 20 June 1623 and died ten days later. Jane Blomely was accused at the Sessions of having 'practised and exercised certain detestable arts called witchcraft and sorcery', which had caused the death of Frances. This information is recorded in the diary of Abraham Pryme, a Yorkshire antiquary of the time who seems to have had a particular interest in witchcraft. He notes that Jane was found guilty

An old
woodcut
of witches
hanging from
the gallows.

by the jury but he gives no indication of what means she was supposed to have employed to bring about this death. Her punishment is not recorded, although, since she was found guilty of causing a death, one would have expected it to be execution.

Pocklington Witches

The parish records of the East Riding market town of Pocklington state that Old Wife Green was burned as a witch in 1630 in the market square. This was not a judicial execution but a mob action. There is no indication of what Old Wife Green had done to drive the citizens of Pocklington to such drastic measures. However, it seems likely that whatever the woman had done, it was considered a serious matter. Perhaps the incident that culminated in her death was but one of many that had gone before. Unless of course this was a case of mob hysteria based on nothing more than rumour and innuendo. It was an action that bestowed on the old woman the unwelcome distinction of being the last person in England to be burned as a witch.

Once again, in 1642, the parish records contain information of a witch in Pocklington. Petronella Haxley, the wife of the blacksmith, was hanged in the marketplace. No mention is made of her actual offence as a witch, nor is there any indication whether this was a hanging based on a local decision. It may well have been an official execution, though it seems surprising that this was not carried out in York in the same way that the execution of Isabella Billington, also of Pocklington, was seven years later. Petronella has gained a curious posthumous fame. In April 2008 a low-budget horror film was released about her. It involves a group of students from the north-east marooned in a house on the moors (though Pocklington actually lies on the edge of the Wolds) who are haunted by Petronella Haxley. In 1643 – the year after Petronella's hanging – the death from bewitchment of a man named Thomas Dobson is recorded in the parish register of Pocklington. Although there is no mention of the name of the witch who struck down Dobson, it would appear that witchcraft was still at work in the little market town.

Janet Burniston, 1639

On 16 December 1639 a special court was held in the church in the village of Kirkby Malzeard near Ripon. Janet Burniston, who stood before it, was accused of having removed and taken home a skull from the churchyard. Since skulls were well-known to be useful ingredients in charms and spells, she was naturally suspected of possible witchery. Janet admitted to the court that she had taken the skull. She explained that she had done so to place it under the head of a certain person named Christopher in order to 'charm him asleep'. This somewhat ambiguous phrase could have a sinister interpretation. However, the court seems to have taken it that Janet meant Christopher no harm. She merely intended to help him to a good night's sleep, albeit by employing a very unusual cure for insomnia. Janet was lucky. She was simply ordered to put the skull back in the place from which she had taken it.

Anthony Ledgard, 1649

Wise men, as we have previously seen, were often sought after for help with everyday troubles. They gained a reputation over a wide area and each had his own particular method intended to impress and add authenticity to his pronouncements. Anthony Ledgard of Heckmondwike was obviously one of the better-educated wise men. He used his knowledge of astrology, or at least of the language of astrology, to convey his advice. Thomas Armitage went to him as 'one who can tell where goods lost or stolne may be founde'. He sought help in locating some wool that had been stolen. Ledgard had his maid bring him an almanac and a book. After making a big show of studying them both carefully he declared that he 'found by the plannetts that itt was of the ayre of water'. He went on to suggest where the wool would be found 'in a taverne or tarnpott covered with much wood'. Ledgard came under investigation in 1649 when these details of his methods were revealed. There is no record of the success or otherwise of these methods, nor of the outcome of the investigation for Ledgard himself. It seems likely that Thomas Armitage himself brought the charge against him out of dissatisfaction with the result of his advice.

Unnamed Man, 1651

Lancelot Milner of Nesfield near Ilkley, in a deposition before a magistrate in 1651, described how an anonymous man 'pretending himself to be dumbe and deafe' came to his house. He stayed there a week and people came from various parts of the country around to consult him. He answered questions from the women regarding love affairs, suitable husbands or the prospect of widowhood. The men wanted to know about stolen goods and horses. All this was done by means of gestures and signs made with a piece of chalk. He did not speak. Since Lancelot Milner was convinced that he was pretending to be deaf and dumb we can only suppose that the novelty of advice given in such a way was his marketing ploy. The recipients of his wisdom seemed for the most part very satisfied by his replies, according to Milner. He was paid with one or two pennies or some ale. Another informant testified that he also gave his advice on occasion without asking for or receiving any reward. A soldier who recognised his accent said that the man came from London. How it came about that he stayed at Lancelot Milner's house when he was unknown to him is not explained (unless perhaps Milner's house was an inn) nor why he felt moved to report him to the authorities. If he was not happy about him plying his trade as a wise man from his house, he could surely have just sent him on his way. He was a long way from his home base and obviously used to travelling around. The story remains a mystery.

Model of a witch in her hovel at Ryedale Folk Museum. (*Lucinda Rennison*)

Mary Hickington, 1651

It may generally seem that the figure of the witch stood alone with the whole community united in the belief in their guilt. Although it was often the case that a kind of hysteria gripped a community once an accusation had been made, and everyone was against the so-called witch, this was not always so. Communities could become divided, with people not only expressing their disbelief but taking positive action to support those accused. In December 1651, a petition was raised with 200 signatories on behalf of Mary Hickington (or Heckington) who was at that time 'a condemned prisoner in York Castle for witchcraft'. Both Mary and her husband were declared by the petitioners to be good and honest citizens, and Mary, the petitioners said, had never been 'in the least wise suspected to be guilty of sorcery or witchcraft or any other misdemeanour not becoming a Christian'. We have seen in previous pages how a petition of fifty names vouching for the good name and character of Susan and Joseph Hinchcliffe proved to be in vain, and how its failure to clear their names led to death. Mary Hickington was more fortunate. An entry in the House of Commons Journal shows that, in March 1652, it was resolved that 'Mary Heckington convicted of Witchcraft be pardoned' and that 'the Clerk of the Commonwealth in Chancery do prepare a Pardon, of course, for her. And that the Lords Commissioners … do pass the said Pardon under the Great Seal accordingly.'

Isabel Emott, 1653

It is understandable that, in the pre-modern age, sickness and death in either people or cattle was so often seen as bewitchment when there was little medical knowledge and doctors and vets were unavailable. Doctors, when they were around, were liable to make matters worse with their blood-letting, and cattle-curers and wise men were the only possible help in the case of sickness in animals. The reasons behind an accusation against a particular person could be more complex. On 14 July 1653, Isabel Emott, the wife of a labourer James Emott of Felwick, was tried at the Sessions at Leeds. She was accused by Richard Longbotham of having bewitched ten of his cows and a black calf that he valued at £40. At that time this was a quite considerable sum, and the fact that Longbotham owned so many cows of such value suggests that he was a man of some substance. Nevertheless, the loss or enfeeblement by sickness of so many valuable beasts would be a great blow for him. Why Isabel Emott was the particular recipient of the accusation of bewitchment is not recorded, nor is the verdict of the court. Perhaps she already had a reputation as a witch or perhaps there was a history of disagreement between her and Longbotham. We shall never know for certain.

Elizabeth Fenwick, 1680

On 11 December 1680, a certain Elizabeth Fenwick was examined before Sir Thomas Loraine on a charge of witchcraft. Her accuser was a Nicolas Rames who

The churchyard at Hinderwell. St Hilda's Well is in the foreground. (*E. Rennison*)

swore under oath that she had threatened him, saying that she would make him repent what he had done. What that was is not on record. Without some knowledge of the status of the two people involved and the relationship between them, we cannot even hazard a guess. It seems obvious though that there had been some kind of 'falling-out' between them. In the deposition made at York Castle, Rames went on to declare that Elizabeth Fenwick had been 'a woman of bad fame for witchcraff severall yeares hearetofore'. His wife, he said, 'lyeing under a sad and lamentable torment of sickness' complained daily that Elizabeth Fenwick tormented and disabled her, leaving her in a state of perplexity. She had seen Fenwick dancing at midnight with the Devil. Despite Nicolas's testimony, Sir Thomas Loraine does not seem to have found it convincing. Elizabeth was acquitted.

A Witch at Hinderwell

In 1708, a young man named Slamper visited a witch in the village of Hinderwell, 10 miles from Whitby. He had quarrelled with his girlfriend and went with a request for the witch to cast a spell on her that would destroy her beauty. The witch agreed to do so and he set off gleefully to return home. His path lay through the churchyard where he was met by a crowd of strange, ghostly figures who set about him with broomsticks. They beat him so severely and so long that he was marked for the rest of his days. The witch had decided to teach him a lesson. The name of the village is thought to be a corruption of Hilda's well from the holy well there. Legend has it that St Hilda refreshed herself from it on her journey to found the Abbey at Whitby in 657. The well is in the churchyard where young Master Slamper met his comeuppance for his unkind and vindictive request. After the repeal of the Witchcraft Act in 1736, when witchcraft was no longer a crime, there was naturally a lack of official records. Belief in witchcraft nevertheless lingered on – especially in remote and country areas – into the 1800s and even the 1900s. Private records such as diaries and the stories collected by Richard Blakeborough in the Guisborough area, as well as Canon Atkinson in Danby, fill the gap up to a point. Relying as they do on the memories of elderly people, they are often incomplete and lacking in detail.

Jane Greer

Little is known of Jane Greer – a supposed witch in Guisborough in the early decades of the nineteenth century – apart from her ability to change into a hare; a useful talent which she shared with other witches on the North York Moors. She was said to have been very beautiful as a young woman. An elegant dancer

An old woodcut of witches cooking up spells.

who showed a dainty ankle, she was pursued by many young men. In old age she seems to have appeared the very stereotype of a witch. She was described as 'ugly as muck wi' black blood in her heart. Old Scrat bought her soul so they say' (Old Scrat was the Devil). It was claimed that she was once chased as a hare by a group of Guisborough men for a distance of 20 miles and still managed to get away. Ugly and old she may have been but even as a hare she still had the men chasing her!

Nanny Thrusk

One of the most powerful and feared tools of a witch was the ability to cast the Evil Eye on victims. The merest glance could immobilise them and make them powerless. It was best to stay well clear of any witch who possessed such a power. If she was met by chance it was wise to avoid looking at her and on no account should one make eye contact. Nanny Thrusk of Bonwick in the East Riding was known to have the Evil Eye. When mischievous boys tried to take away her donkey in order to amuse themselves, Nanny caught them. She transfixed them with a glance. There they were held until she felt inclined to let them go. It was not the first time that Nanny had used her special gift. She had done penance in nearby Skipsea Church several times for such tricks. Barefooted, dressed only in a shroud-like sheet and carrying a candle, she was obliged to walk up the aisle before the congregation and listen to a sermon calling on her to repent. This was a common form of penance at that time used as a punishment for other sins such as adultery. It seems to have had little effect in this case. Nanny does not appear to have been at all penitent or deterred by this humiliation. Perhaps she just couldn't help doing what she did. Perhaps she enjoyed it!

Sally Carey

A young married couple from Kirby Hill near Boroughbridge were looking forward to the birth of their first child when by chance they met the witch Sally Carey near the Devil's Arrows, three huge standing stones on the edge of the town. She shook her stick fiercely at them and, to their surprise, screamed that, although they wanted a boy, she would see to it that the baby was a girl. It was a mystery to them as to what they might have done to annoy her, but sure enough when the baby arrived it was a girl. The couple made the best of their disappointment and hoped that a second child would be the longed-for son and heir. Sadly, some months after the second baby was expected, the husband was thrown from his horse and killed. Late in the evening, shortly after this sad event, Sally appeared at the widow's house and screamed at her, 'It shan't be a lad this tahme, nawther.' This so terrified the mother-to-be that she collapsed and was unable to do anything for a time. She was eventually persuaded by her friends to consult a wise man at nearby Aldborough to seek his aid in removing the witch's power. He did his best at midnight in a tightly closed room with a black cock roasted on a fire of rowan branches, and a special incantation. He succeeded in that the baby was a boy, but

A nineteenth-century illustration of a witch in a ducking stool.

alas, he was born crippled with a crooked back. Another visit to the wise man assured the heart-broken mother that if she did not remarry in the next seven years all would be well; the boy would grow strong and his back would straighten, and so it turned out. But as the old lady who told Richard Blakeborough of this witch in the late 1800s said, 'T'aud witch tried all maks an' manders o' ways ti git her ti wed … Sha war awlus sending some good leeaking chap for ti tice her bud sha kept single, an' bested t'aud witch in t'end.'

Mary Marshall

'Nobbut an old meddling piece of nowt' was the description of Mary Marshall at the beginning of the twentieth century by those who remembered her in the 1800s. She was noted for cursing and bewitching people and causing devastation among their animals and crops. If any cow became wasted and failed to thrive, Mary was sure to be blamed. If the crops were spoiled by the blight, once again it must be Mary's wicked work. One person who suffered from Mary's ill-wishing was perhaps not entirely undeserving of it. When she met a Stokesley man named Morton who was well-known to have perjured himself to save a friend from a murder charge, he was unwise enough to treat Mary with rude disdain. He told her brusquely to get out of his way and called her a 'spawn of the Devil'. She fixed him with her eye as he gazed scornfully down on her from his horse and said, 'As you fall from your horse you shall fall in fortune. As your horse runs so shall your wealth.' The horse promptly threw its rider and galloped off. Nothing went well for Morton from that day as Mary's curse took its effect. As Mary grew older she lost her wits and took to crowing like a cock. Where we today might think in terms of dementia the good folk of Stokesley were sure it was the result of her dealings with the Devil.

Nanny Appleby

Witches in North Yorkshire are often known as 'Nanny This' or 'Nanny That'. This is not their Christian name but a title. Children today often call their grandmother Nan, Nanna or Nanny, a version of Granny, which in its turn is often used in a general way to indicate the age of the recipient. This is the case with the witches to whom it is attached. As we know, old women were often regarded as witches. One such was Nanny Appleby who lived on Dalton Moor. Nanny was often called on to help people rid themselves of curses and spells, though little is known of her doings. On one occasion she was called in to the seriously ill son of a widow from Aldfield. Nanny declared that he was possessed by the Devil and set about driving it out. This seems to have entailed a great deal of noise, shrieks and crashing of furniture and smashing of crockery. The Devil must have put up a terrible fight but was finally beaten by Nanny. Unfortunately, though she had driven it out she seems to have been unable to send it back to wherever it had come from. It entered instead the body of a lad called Tom Moss who was found drowned a month later. Was this an accident or was he driven to take his own life by the Devil? Nanny Appleby did not like Tom, but it does seem extraordinarily unkind of her if she deliberately sent the Devil to take him over. The widow's son was completely cured of his illness and made a rapid recovery.

Religion Against Bewitchment

As we have seen elsewhere, for truly religious people their first defence against witchcraft was their faith in the power of God. Oliver Heywood, a nonconformist minister who lived from 1630 to 1712, noted in his autobiography a perfect example of this in a case concerning a twelve-year-old boy who had long been ill 'under a strange and sad hand of God in his body'. His parents did not immediately conclude that he was bewitched although many others did. They consulted a doctor who told them that what their son was suffering from was not a natural ailment, but he 'hath had some hurt by an evel tongue'. Even doctors at the time were not always immune from the belief in bewitchment and were prepared to offer what were more like spells than medicine to cure it. This particular one went on to recommend a very strange prescription. The parents were to make a cake or loaf from wheat meal mixed with the boy's water and containing some of his hair and 'horse-shooe stumps'. This was then to be burned on the fire. Recognising that this was in the nature of a charm or spell, and fearing that as such it was against their religion and an offence to God, the mother went to the Revd Heywood for advice. He was aware of the superstition that following these instructions would reveal the witch who had caused the illness and bring her to them. He was not happy about it and consulted with a colleague. They both agreed 'it not to be any way of God, having no foundation either in nature or divine revelation in scripture'. His advice to the parents was that they should seek the help of God by fasting and prayer. This they agreed to do in company with the minister. Whether their prayers were answered is not made plain.

Witches Today

Witches are a thing of the past. True? Well, 'Yes' and 'No'. We may feel fairly certain that malicious witchcraft with intent to harm is indeed a thing of the past, but there are still people who believe that there are special powers that they are able to use for good, to help both themselves and others.

Known variously as White Witches, Crafters or Wiccans, many are pleased simply to call themselves 'witches' and their practices 'witchcraft'. They look back to the religion of pagan times. Wicca, which takes its name from the Old English word for a witch, is a religious movement developed in England in the first half of the twentieth century. It is duotheistic, with a Goddess and her spouse, the horned God. There are different denominations within the movement, known as Traditions, and named after the influential primary figures. The Gardnerian Tradition, for example, takes its name from Gerald Gardner, the Wiccan High Priest, who was instrumental in popularising Wicca in the 1950s. Not all these Traditions actually use the name of Wicca. However, respect for nature in all its aspects is at the heart of their beliefs, no matter what name they choose to give themselves. Festivals based on the seasons – sometimes referred to as Sabbats – are celebrated throughout the year, usually twice in each season. The rituals reflect the ceremonial magic of earlier centuries.

Spells and divinations are a part of Wiccan practice, but the use of them to harm, manipulate or control a person in any way is strictly forbidden. There are strong and explicit rules, known as the Wiccan Rede, which must be respected and adhered to. The followers of this Neo-Pagan witchcraft believe that their religion is very real and powerful. It may be used for others in, for instance, healing or for personal achievement in relationships and business.

So are there witches still in Yorkshire? A quick trawl of the internet shows that there are witchcraft groups, or 'covens', throughout the county with headquarters in Leeds. Pat Crowther, the Sheffield-born author of the book

Witchcraft in Yorkshire, published in 1973 by Dalesman, was an important figure in the early promotion of Wicca through books, radio talks and articles in newspapers and magazines. She was initiated into the sect by the High Priest, Gerald Gardner himself.

Time Chart

It is not always possible to be absolutely accurate in dating the stories told in these pages, particularly the later ones when the witches involved were not brought before any legal authority.

1286	Godfrey Darel, Rievaulx Abbey
1488–1561	Old Mother Shipton, Knaresborough
1538	Mabel Brigge, Holmpton, East Yorkshire
1570	Lady Jane Cholmeley, Whitby
1594	Cuthbert Williamson, York
1597	Elizabeth Melton, Collingham, near Wetherby
1603	Mary Pannell, Castleford
1605	Joan Jurdie, Rossington, near Doncaster
1612	Jennet Preston, Gisburn, West Yorkshire
1621	The Timble Witches, Timble, Craven District
1623	Jane Blomeley, Doncaster
	Elizabeth Creary, Northallerton
1639	Janet Burniston, Kirkby Malzeard, near Ripon
1642	Petronella Haxley, Pocklington
1646	Elizabeth Crossley, Heptonstall
1649	Isabella Billington, Pocklington
	Jane Kighly, Idle, West Riding
	Anthony Ledgard, Heckmondwike
1650	Margaret Morton, Kirkthorpe, West Riding
	Mary Sykes, Bowling, near Bradford

1651	Mary Hickington
1652	Richard Breare and others, Mirfield, near Wakefield
	Hester France, Huddersfield
	Anne Hunnam (Marchant), Scarborough
1653	Isabel Emott, Felwick
	Ann Greene, Gargrave
	Elizabeth Lambe, Reedness, near Goole
1654	Elizabeth Roberts, Beverley
	William and Mary Wade, Ripon
1655	Katherine Earle, Rothwell, West Riding
1656	Jennet and George Benson, Newton, near Wakefield
1657	Thomas and Mary Jefferson, Woodhouse, Sheffield
1664	Anne Huson, Doll Bilby, Burton Agnes, East Riding
1670	Anne Wilkinson, Alne, near Easingwold
1674	Susan Hinchcliffe, Denby, West Riding
1680	Elizabeth Fenwick, Longwitton
1736	Bridget and Margaret Goldsbrough, Baildon
1750–80	Old Nanny, Great Ayton
b. 1765	Nan Hardwick, Spittlehouses, Danby Dale
1775–1800s	Old Kathy, Ruswarp, near Whitby
1785	Hannah Green, Yeadon
1800–1810	Old Sally Kindreth, Scorton, near Richmond
1809	Mary Bateman, Leeds
d. 1826	Susannah Gore, Driffield
d. 1835	Peggy Flounders, Marske, North Riding
1800s–1900s	Wise men, Widespread
	Molly Cass, Leeming N. Riding
	Jane Greer, Guisborough
	Nanny Thrusk, Bonwick, E. Riding
	Sally Carey, Boroughbridge
	Mary Marshall, Stokesley
	Nanny Appleby, Dalton Moor, N. Riding
	Nanny Pierson, Goathland N. York Moors
1830	Hannah Waugh, Broughton, Northallerton

Bibliography

There have been many books published over the years on witches and witchcraft. A comprehensive bibliography of titles just on witchcraft in Yorkshire would run to several pages. Here is a small selection of those books that I have found particularly useful while writing this book.

Blakeborough, R., *Wit, Character, Folklore & Customs of the North Riding of Yorkshire*, Wakefield: EP Publishing, 1973 (reprint of work first published in 1898).

Ewen, C. L'Estrange, *Witchcraft and Demonianism*, London: Frederick Muller, 1970 (Facsimile edition of book first published in 1933).

Lumby, J., *The Lancashire Witch-Craze: Jennet Preston and the Lancashire Witches 1612*, Lancaster: Carnegic Publishing, 1995.

Martin, L., *The History of Witchcraft*, Harpenden: Pocket Essentials, 2002.

Peach, H., *Curious Tales from West Yorkshire*, Stroud: The History Press, 2010.

Raine, J. (ed), *Depositions from the Castle of York Relating to Offenses Committed in the Northern Counties in the Seventeenth Century*, London: Surtees Society, 1860 (available to read online at the Internet Archive).

Sharpe, J. A., *Witchcraft in Seventeenth-Century Yorkshire: Accusations and Counter Measures (University of York Borthwick Paper No. 81)*, York: Borthwick Institute of Historical Research, 1992.

Walker, P. N., *Murders and Mysteries from the North York Moors*, London: Robert Hale, 1988.

Williams, M., *Witchcraft in Old North Yorkshire*, Beverley: Hutton Press, 1987.

Acknowledgements

My thanks are due to the following people:

My son Nick Rennison for his unfailing help and encouragement during the writing of this book. My daughter Lucinda Rennison for her technical expertise and assistance. Eve Gorton for her invaluable help with research. Graham Eagland for his excellent photographs of several places associated with the witches in this book, and his map of Yorkshire. Roger Nelson for his interest in the project and for his suggestions of witches who might be included. The Whitby Literary & Philosophical Society for permission to reproduce photographs of Old Kathy Doll and Splintwork from the Whitby Museum.